How to Lose Everything in Politics
Except Massachusetts

How to Lose Everything in Politics Except Massachusetts

by Kristi Witker

 Mason & Lipscomb PUBLISHERS   NEW YORK

For Alvin

Contents

List of Photographs

x ☐

How to Lose Everything in Politics
Except Massachusetts

chapter 1

Fitting the Wheels
on the Bandwagon

On Wednesday, October 25, 1972, I sat beside Frank
Mankiewicz, George McGovern's Political Director, on
a flight from Washington to Detroit. The sky was gray,
the flight bumpy, the stewardess harassed, and the
magazine rack bare with the exception of one limp
copy of August's *Today's Health*.

"I guess it's all over," I said.

"Over?" Frank's bushy eyebrows shot up. "No way."
He swiveled around in his seat, adding six more wrinkles to his already crumpled shirt. "You don't know the
latest . . . This is gonna break tomorrow. You know
Nixon's top man, H. R. Haldeman, who's been linked to
the Watergate but who's denied it, right? Well, we've
just found out this same guy was implicated after Nixon's 1962 and '68 campaigns for carrying on all sorts of
political sabotage against Pat Brown and Hubert Humphrey!"

"I don't think anyone cares about Watergate," I said
sadly. "Can't we come up with a different sort of scandal—a vicuna coat or something?"

Frank shook his head. "You just don't understand
politics," he said. "This isn't your average year." He
leaned forward, lit a cigarette, and looked very intense.
"The polls don't mean a damn thing. Everything's go-

☐ 3

ing for McGovern now, and when this latest news breaks tomorrow—well, you'll see. We're gonna make it. I really think we're gonna make it."

It didn't cheer me up. After nine months of working for George McGovern, I felt nothing. It seemed, in fact, like an interminable time spent in the dentist's chair. I didn't care what happened anymore. I just wanted it all to stop.

And thank God it would—in just thirteen days.

It had all started in February 1972, in Switzerland, where I had been enjoying an exceptionally pleasant ski vacation at St. Moritz. I was sound asleep one morning at 4 a.m. when the telephone rang joltingly in my ear. It was a bad connection from Manchester, New Hampshire. And on the other end was a tired-voiced Pierre Salinger. Why not give up this life of obvious decadence, he said, and do something meaningful— like come to New Hampshire and work for George McGovern.

It sounded like a nice idea for after the ski season, but Pierre was persistent. So I got up and looked at myself very seriously in the mirror and said, O.K., for three years, you've been bitching about Richard Nixon and inequality and not having a voice in the government, and now, what are you going to do about it? I was tempted to say "very little" and crawl back to bed, but this was my big chance to do something meaningful, so I said yes to Pierre, and he said, "Come right away."

A day later, I took a 6 a.m. train to Zurich and raced to the airport for the nonstop flight to Boston. That is, it was a nonstop flight for the people who were actually on the plane. I wasn't. For me, the airline had made a tiny little computer error, routing me on another flight by way of Toronto with a change of planes that would land me in Boston at midnight instead of the originally scheduled 5 p.m. This tiny computer error did not, however, apply to my luggage, which traveled to Boston at 5 and awaited me in several tattered sections. Through no fault of the airline, I was informed by Boston's Baggage Claims Office at 1:00 a.m., my skiis had apparently plunged out of their ski bag in midflight, leaving the bag in shreds and everything I'd stuffed in it—like my favorite fur mittens and fur hat—in thin air. Oh well, why get upset—it was only trivia, and I was on my way to something much more important.

Since I was on the wrong flight, it was 1:00 in the morning and a blizzard was raging outside, George McGovern was not waiting to meet me—nor was anyone else—nor, understandably, was there anyone around the airport at that predawn hour interested in driving me through the mounting drifts to Manchester. But finally, one taxi driver agreed to do so for a meager $60. And so, at 4:30 a.m., I arrived in Manchester, New Hampshire, a 23-hour journey from the Palace Hotel to Howard Johnson's Motel. A note from Pierre Salinger at the front desk informed me that he had gone up north somewhere to give a speech. "Welcome to New Hampshire," it said. "You'll love it."

My campaign had begun.

There was an air of excitement in the motel—the beginning of a campaign "season," reminiscent of the first day of school each year when everything seemed clean and fresh and new and you couldn't wait to catch up on your friends' summer vacations and tell them about your own. Suddenly in New Hampshire, many old friends of the 1968 campaign were back. Later on, of course, it would be just like school, the same tired, pale faces, the same worn books and corridors, the same yearning for a vacation just to get away from it all, but now everything was new and the campaign was, after all, the biggest story in town.

Days were cold, gray, and snowy which made Howard Johnson's cosier, and people were all indoors and easy to find—CBS, McGovern, and his staff at Howard Johnson's; NBC at the jazzier but less convenient Sheraton Wayfarer; Muskie and his staff at the downtown Sheraton Carpenter.

McGovern rated only 26% in the Boston Globe's February poll, 19% according to The Public Television Service of New Hampshire, but the mood was one of impending possibility. We had nowhere to go but up and after all, we weren't trying to *win* the New Hampshire primary since Muskie was naturally top dog in the yard next to his own. We just wanted to do well enough not to look ridiculous, and that was possible.

The first couple of days I met some of the McGovern aides, all of whom seemed easygoing and relatively humorous. There was Frank Mankiewicz, an old friend, a former Director of the Peace Corps, Washington columnist, and Robert Kennedy's 1968 press secretary, who was national campaign director; Gary Hart, a 34-year-old Denver lawyer and former Robert Kennedy coordinator in the Rocky Mountain states who was campaign manager and who looked a bit like Warren Beatty; Kirby Jones, press secretary, a short, smiling former Peace Corps volunteer and Robert Kennedy worker; Gordon Weil, 35, a serious-looking dark-haired economist who had worked as executive assistant on McGovern's Senate staff for four years, who had started out as campaign press secretary and had now become

6 □

traveling advisor; Shirley MacLaine, the actress; Pete Hamill, busily turning out pro-McGovern articles for the *New York Post;* photographer Lee Goff; and Dick Tuck, the talented practical joker from Bobby Kennedy's campaign. It held promise of being at least an intellectually sexy campaign.

To learn about New Hampshire, I joined Pierre in the northern town of Berlin to work for several days with a girl from Swarthmore, Pennsylvania, on a college leave of absence as a McGovern volunteer. Pierre said we wouldn't do well in Berlin, a town almost obscured by the smoke of the Brown Paper Company which, being the town's main employer, apparently felt little compulsion to adopt even the most minimal pollution controls.

Berlin was not, as they say, "into" the primary. On street after street, Pierre would walk up to people saying, "Hello, I'm Pierre Salinger and I hope you'll support George McGovern in the primary on March 7th." No response. I couldn't tell whether they didn't know who Salinger was, didn't know McGovern, didn't like McGovern, didn't know there was a primary—or for that matter, even what a primary was. Whatever the reason, the result was uncheery. The three of us went to two dinners in Berlin—one at the Kiwanis Club and one at the Elks. We even stopped in at the American Legion where Indiana Senator Vance Hartke, who had hopes, albeit waning, for the nomination, offered me a job working in his campaign—for money, but no one seemed impressed with George McGovern. So far, it didn't strike me that my presence in New Hampshire was exactly crucial, but at least I'd learned where Berlin was and had met a very nice girl from Swarthmore.

Back to Howard Johnson's, only not exactly. They

□ 7

were very sorry, but CBS needed my room, and they knew I'd understand but I no longer had one. I didn't understand, of course, but after calling nearly everyone in town, I finally maneuvered a day bed in a room next to the bar at the Queen City Motel, this one availability occasioned by the motel's almost inaccessible position atop an iced-over, perpendicular driveway. Fortunately, I soon discovered that if I could get a car with chains to haul me up at night, I could, by clutching tree branches along the driveway's edge, slide myself down in the morning.

One morning, having slid into Howard Johnson's, I was having breakfast with a couple of friends when George McGovern walked in. He was alone and looking for a table, but at that moment all were taken. Sitting there in a formica booth, it seemed unthinkable to us that a potential Presidential candidate should have to circle the coffee shop floor until such time as he could make a clear pounce on an unoccupied table, so one of the reporters leaned out of our cubicle and asked if he'd like to join us. McGovern came over and seemed genuinely pleased by the invitation. It was the People's Campaign all right.

That day Pierre asked me to accompany him to Merv Weston's advertising and public relations agency to hear some new commercials. The first was a radio spot, a recording made by Bobby Kennedy several years before, saying that he'd found George McGovern to be the most decent man in the Senate. It gave me a creepy feeling. "It looks like McGovern is nothing on his own, that he has to rely on the Kennedy ghost," I said. The opinion was not shared, and I regretted having opened my mouth. The television commercials, however, were good, managing very effectively and with seemingly

8 □

little artiface, to portray McGovern to the viewer just as he came across in person—a calm, compassionate man who *listened* to people and cared about their problems.

But there was one of them that just missed. Actually, it missed by a lot. In it, McGovern was talking about the War with some wounded veterans, one of whom spoke very bitterly about losing his legs and getting no help from the government. When the veteran finished speaking, McGovern turned to him, and in a voice which could only be described as nasal-clergical, remarked, "You love this country—there's no question about that—and yet, you are about halfway mad at it, too. Aren't you?"

Halfway mad at it? Good God! The man had no legs! Loathe and hate would be more like it. What was needed here was outrage, not a sermon. I said so. But no one agreed. You don't understand about commercials, they said.

The next day Frank Mankiewicz gave me my assignment. I was to run a voter analysis, that is, pick out some 40 voter precincts across the state and write up statistics on them, including such information as ethnic backgrounds, income levels, type of employment, and past voting records of the residents. I would work with local campaign coordinators, volunteers, and a Harvard senior, and polling wizard Pat Caddell to prepare a key precinct analysis on election night which would be used to background newspapers and television stations and to show McGovern and his top advisers the early voting trends. Somehow, I would also arrange to have reliable poll watchers from across the state phone me with this information on special phones set up for my personal use on election night.

Campaign storefronts are naturally labyrinthian places, full of dusty corners, overflowed ashtrays, and half-empty Coke bottles, sorely lacking in telephones, chairs, typewriters, desks, space, and oxygen, and this one was no exception. Not knowing the state (except Berlin) nor the names of any McGovern coordinators, I found the prospect of the job rather awesome and wondered quite seriously what became of AWOL campaign workers.

After getting that assignment, I didn't see much of New Hampshire because I rarely left headquarters, but one day, having called 32 people, 31 of whom had "gone out somewhere," "gone home but doesn't have a telephone," "gone to do an errand for her mother," or "stopped working here last month," I decided to see the outdoors and take a look at McGovern's competition.

Camera in hand, I wandered over to Muskie's headquarters at the Sheraton Carpenter Hotel and found myself on a bus filled with reporters heading out with Muskie to the Edison Electronics factory. Muskie had been endlessly likened to Abe Lincoln by the press, but up close, he looked not craggy, but weary. And unlike Lincoln, who finally came around to a definite opinion on slavery, Muskie, in the six speeches I had heard during this campaign, couldn't seem to come around to a definite opinion on anything, except perhaps how many times he had visited New Hampshire. Twenty-three times I think it was. Immediately I was struck by the differences in the two candidate's staffs. Muskie men seemed instinctively to button all three buttons on their dark gray suit jackets, and they seemed older, more organized, and slightly arrogant, the kind of people who are involved in a job which promises great rewards because their man is the one everyone says will win. This afternoon they were very intense and carried briefcases because, after the factory stop they were accompanying Muskie to a northern New Hampshire town where he would give another speech.

At the factory, we piled out of the bus and straggled into Edison Electronics' waiting room. Muskie strode in on our heels, and after the usual factory-entering formalities (shaking hands with the manager and the manager's assistant and posing for the company photographer, who had unfortunately selected for his big moment a Polaroid camera with a faulty flash), the candidate vanished into the factory. We followed. Crunch. My way was suddenly barred by a Muskie press aide with an excessive amount of teeth. "Only four reporters in with the Senator," he snarled. An Australian reporter for the *Sydney Morning Herald* objected. What was the point, he asked, quite reasonably I thought, of hauling a busload of reporters to a remote factory to stand in the hall? "Only four reporters in with the Senator," the aide said again, apparently unable to grasp the question. It suddenly reminded me of the last day of a high-geared Presidential campaign. Only this was an ordinary day of a low-geared first of 23 primaries. Smiling at him vacantly and clutching my camera, I pushed by. Eleven reporters followed.

The factory consisted of rows and rows of enormously long tables with stools on which sat rows and rows of men and women (more women) doing something very complicated with little wires. And Ed Muskie came alive. He loped down the aisles. "I'm Ed Muskie," he said, draping himself over a worker's back and hugging him in a statesman-bear sort of way. "I hope you'll vote for me."

☐ *11*

We came to the end of one aisle. For an instant, Muskie looked lost, pondering which way to turn. And then he trotted down the aisle to the left, sometimes shaking hands but mostly hugging and squeezing. It struck me as just a little too tactile. Down one aisle, up another, up, down. Our little band of reporters padded after him, but his eyes never met ours. Muskie was wearing a light gray knit suit and short brown boots, into the left one of which his pant leg had unfortunately crept, giving him a somewhat peg-legged appearance. I wanted to tell him before he traveled the next 37 aisles, but the eyes of his aides put me off. I said nothing.

It seemed very likely that 410 votes would be literally squeezed out of the workers at Edison Electronics Corporation, but I was not impressed. I was *de*pressed. It was somehow less than I had expected from the man "with the only chance to beat Nixon." But I decided something at that moment. McGovern might lose New Hampshire but he would win the nomination mainly because he had no real competition. I bet $100 on it with a young free-lance photographer from Massachusetts. He gave me 10 to 1 odds—a lucky thing. I later lived on that money during a long, hot summer of campaign blues in Washington.

In New Hampshire, everything seemed to be going right for McGovern and wrong for Muskie. Where McGovern's mistakes were largely ignored, Muskie's were published. On February 24, a letter was printed in the *Manchester Union Leader,* written by one Paul Morrison from Florida who claimed that Muskie had referred to French-Canadians as "Canucks." The commotion that resulted (a large segment of New Hampshire voters being of French-Canadian ancestry) forced

12 □

Muskie to interrupt his campaign schedule in Florida and return to New Hampshire to refute the charges. There, standing on that flatbed truck in front of the newspaper's offices, he berated publisher William Loeb for the Canuck charge, and then overcome by frustration and fatigue, wept over what to him was the last straw, an unflattering interview with his wife, Jane, also printed in the paper.

Rumors constantly filtered into our headquarters that Muskie was having other bad breaks. Apparently, New Hampshire was being blitzed by phone calls from late-working "Muskie pollsters" who had a proclivity for dialing the same households three and four times in succession, asking the same questions. And another group of post-midnight callers was at work identifying themselves as members of the "Harlem for Muskie Committee," assuring New Hampshire voters that Muskie would bring about "full justice for black people."

It wasn't going much better for him in Florida. Letters on phony "Citizens for Muskie" stationery, with Muskie's signature, flooded that state, calling attention to some rather bizarre sexual behavior on the part of Muskie's major opponents, Senators Hubert Humphrey and Henry Jackson. Another batch of Muskie letters, slipped under the windshield wipers of cars parked at a huge Wallace rally near St. Petersburg, warned, "If you like Hitler, you'll love Wallace." Billboards mysteriously popped up, sponsored by "Mothers for Muskie," urging "more busing," and once again, the midnight callers were at work, enraging a large assortment of previously Muskie-inclined voters.

As word of these events spread through our small New Hampshire campaign office, there was mixed reaction—laughter, of course, but also nervousness. Who was doing these things? Was it Humphrey, Jackson, Wallace, or us? If it was the McGovern campaign, it would mean to me that I'd interrupted a Swiss vacation for a decidedly less worthy cause than that aboveboard People's Campaign I'd been so excited about. Also, if we were responsible, our victims would eventually pay us back in kind, which could make all our work meaningless. Even if we weren't doing it, it would mean that whoever was, could always turn their attentions to us. It was unnerving no matter how you looked at it.

There were others at our campaign office, though, who thought a little political sabotage a good thing and who were quick to take credit for the work itself or at least some prior knowledge of it. Several campaign workers admitted in amplified tones, that although they couldn't go into it, they knew our campaign had a spy "very high up" in the Muskie campaign who had been helpful in "liberating" some key documents as well as coordinating some "unfortunate events." It all pointed to Dick Tuck, the practical joker of the Kennedy campaign.

But Tuck certainly wasn't working high up in the Muskie operation. He was too well known, and he was also prominently in evidence at the McGovern press suite bar. Perhaps he was the coordinator of the unfortunate events. But that didn't seem likely either, because only one of these events had the Dick Tuck touch. That was the coffee klatsch opening of Muskie's New Hampshire campaign headquarters, where guests chugging down their last swallow of coffee gazed into the bottom of their cups to see the words "McGovern for President."

14 □

Tuck's specialty was a kind of intellectual humor, with good visual effects, where the victim was embarrassed, not destroyed. What was happening in New Hampshire wasn't visual, wasn't funny, and *was* destructive.

On March 1, however, it seemed for the first time that maybe some of the unfortunate events were catching up with us. That day, some 185,000 New Hampshire Democrats and Independents opened their mail to find letters from "United Democrats for Kennedy" urging them to ignore the announced candidates on primary day and write in Ted Kennedy's name. "Every poll demonstrates that Kennedy is the one Democrat who will surely beat Richard Nixon in November," the letter declared; and, "if the citizens of New Hampshire call for him to lead us by writing in his name on the Democratic ballot, that example will be followed by millions of Americans across the country. And Senator Kennedy *will* answer our call."

It was signed by one Robin Ficker, a 28-year-old lobbyist and candidate for Congress in Maryland, who announced in a hurriedly assembled press conference at Howard Johnson's that he was heading the Draft-Kennedy Movement, and implied, while undergoing a massive attack of hand trembling and perspiration, that Kennedy was favorably inclined toward his action. Kennedy, of course, disavowed anything to do with Ficker, but who was behind it? Some said it had to be McGovern because local opinion seemed to be that a Kennedy write-in could cost Muskie three votes to every one lost by McGovern.

But it was more logical to assume that those behind the write-in might be the two Conservative candidates, Wilbur Mills, Chairman of the House Ways and Means

Committee, and Sam Yorty, Mayor of Los Angeles. After all, Kennedy would draw votes away from *both* liberals, Muskie and McGovern, to the benefit of Yorty and Mills. And why would McGovern want to lose *any* votes to Kennedy?

From the beginning of his campaign, McGovern had been fighting his image as a Kennedy "stalking horse" —a man in the race with Kennedy workers just to get the cart rolling before the true candidate, Ted Kennedy, jumped in the driver's seat. Bringing Kennedy into the race, no matter how, could only increase the stalking-horse image. There had to be someone more powerful than Robin Ficker, Yorty, or Mills behind this extremely well-financed but unauthorized campaign.

Pierre seemed visibly worried, enough so that he asked me to phone Kennedy's press secretary, Dick Drayne, in Washington and arrange for an amplified long-distance call to come through from Kennedy during the press conference, denouncing Ficker's move. The telephone was set up, reporters stood by, but the call from Kennedy never came.

It was a symbolic moment, one which would recur many times again before the end of the campaign. We would never be able to shake off the Kennedy ghost. Instead, it would become more haunting, more crippling, always affecting McGovern's major decisions. Later, in Miami, even with the nomination in his hand, McGovern would still be waiting for Kennedy's call.

In New Hampshire, whether it knew it or not, the press was plugging McGovern. On March 5, two days before the primary, the Sunday *New York Times* featured an article filed in Chicago by correspondent R. W.

16 ☐

(Johnny) Apple, which began, "Sen. Edmund S. Muskie's drive for the Democratic Presidential nomination has begun to flag with the onset of the primary election season, which opens with Tuesday's vote in New Hampshire. . . ." Everything seemed to be working for us.

The big event was to be a television debate that Sunday night between all the contenders: McGovern, Muskie, Yorty, Hartke, and Edward Coll, a 32-year-old Connecticut social worker, who although too young to be elected President, had maneuvered himself onto the ballot, he said, to campaign for better treatment of the poor. We all got into a rickety, cold bus and headed for Durham University for the live, closed-circuit telecast. Shirley MacLaine and Pete Hamill sat behind me, and Shirley announced that she was giving up acting for a year to work for McGovern. He was the only candidate who could bring change, she said, and change was what was wanted by the rich, the poor, but especially the middle class, the group that had lost the most and, therefore, had the most to gain. I admired her dedication.

The debate turned out to be four sermons and a rat. Interrupting such pontifications as "I speak for the heart and soul of America" (Hartke), "I believe in prayer and have practiced it all my life" (Muskie), "Our objective in Vietnam is honorable" (Yorty), and "There's no way for the President to earn public trust unless he trusts the public" (McGovern), Ned Coll suddenly pulled from his pocket a huge lifelike rubber rat. Waving it at the TV screen and his startled audience, he yelled, "We can't do anything in this country until we do something about the rat!" He was righter than I realized then.

□ 17

The rented Xerox machine broke on Election Day. Frank Mankiewicz wanted ten copies of all the precinct sheets I had prepared, which meant he wanted 400 pages, a relatively difficult thing to accomplish without a copier. I, therefore, remember little of our first big primary day except the Xerox repairman. But he was one man who came through when it mattered, and our election returns rolled in. Then all we had to do was put together a press release saying how well McGovern had done in each area—"doing well in middle class suburbs, better than expected with French-Canadians, showing surprising strength in blue-collar wards," and so forth. The press bought the whole show, and the next day it was all in print. And we were as surprised as anyone. In fact, that unexpected blue-collar strength in New Hampshire changed the strategy of the campaign. From now on, said Frank, my main emphasis should be the blue-collar vote—to point out that, contrary to public opinion, the bulk of McGovern's strength was *not* suburbanites and college students, but the working middle class.

Most of the press, Frank, and the McGoverns flew back to Washington from Manchester on a bouncy chartered flight during which, I later heard, 75% of the strapped-in guests turned almost indelibly green. I, however, had the good sense to drive to Boston in a comfortable car with two New York friends and Pierre, who, during the ride, asked me to stay on as key precinct analyst without salary but with paid travel expenses. The next primary would be a warm one, Florida. I agreed, and flew back to New York with my bagless skiis, an enormous pile of key precinct analyses, and a very good feeling about the McGovern campaign.

Friends, having heard I was working for McGovern,

said "Congratulations." This was rather significant, I thought, because, of course, we'd lost (Muskie with 46% of the vote to our 37%). Later, McGovern aides would always refer to our New Hampshire "victory," and it was this attitude, I think, buoyed by the press that helped us *really* begin to win.

chapter 2

A Once-in-a-Lifetime Opportunity

To continue working for McGovern would mean exhausting my meager savings, but I reasoned that since I believed in George McGovern's stands on the war and the economy, it was worth it. He was the underdog who could only win if everyone who felt as I did got out and really helped. At least, I would be undertaking something with a lot more purpose than anything I'd done in the past.

For a year, I had been existing rather uncomfortably as a free-lance writer-photographer, having given up a secure, safe, and pleasant job as an editor and writer at *American Heritage* magazine. Before that, I'd had a rather spotted career trying to decide what I wanted to be when I grew up.

After college, I had sailed off to Japan where I lived with a Japanese family and acted, badly and briefly, in a series of Japanese movies. My starring role was in a two-minute segment in Toho Production's *Battle in Outer Space*, where I played the sister of a Japanese spacegirl about to leave for the moon. All I had to do as she stepped into the rocket was say two sentences in Japanese and burst into tears. It was not a difficult role, especially as the temperature outside next to the rocket that day was 34°, and I, dressed in sleeveless gabardine, was so cold and miserable I was about to burst into tears anyway. I also played with great distinction the devoted wife of a wounded serviceman in *Hey Pineapple*. Then my big chance had come. A cigar-smoking producer from Allied Artists had traveled all the way from Los Angeles to Tokyo and offered me a part in *From Hell to Eternity* (not *From Here to Eternity*, sadly). The part, however, involved denuding myself from the waist up at some important point in the script, and all I could think of was those cold Japanese studios (light came through an open skylight over an unheated room), masses of goose bumps, and feeling foolish. I turned it down.

Next, I worked in New York as gal Friday for the actress, Mary Martin. My job there was to plan her daughter's wedding. That was fun because she had a beautiful apartment overlooking the East River, and I love weddings. I planned and planned, ordered reams of invitations and flowers, and then her daughter suddenly eloped. So I had to unplan the wedding, which took considerably more time and offered minimal rewards. Cartier was indignant, the florist snarled, the River Club was wild—all at *me*, and I hadn't even eloped.

So I tried my hand at modeling and television. Naturally, I auditioned for more commercials than I got; the one that particularly stands out being one for Ban deodorant, where I almost got the chance to be one of two girls in a locker room sniffing away at my Ban-laden armpit with overwhelming happiness, but at just the vital sniff, I collapsed in giggles to the great displeasure of the account executive.

My stage career was similarly short. I played the waitress in *Tall Story*, an off-Broadway play (quite far off

22 ☐

Broadway, at that—East 77th Street, I think it was) about basketball players. Most of the action took place in a bar with the various characters sitting about talking. Obviously, they had to drink something while they endlessly sat there, so they needed a waitress. I was it. They would call me (my stage name was Hazel), I'd come out and take their orders, fill up appropriate glasses on the floor in a tiny offstage alcove, and bring out the glasses on a tray. I carried the tray brilliantly. Irene Selznick was coming opening night, and I was sure I'd be discovered for Hollywood where I obviously belonged. But opening night a very sad thing happened. Just as I was taking my first order, there was this awful crash. In my dark and cluttered alcove, some klutz had walked on my tray. There was nothing I could do. I served the basketball players a trayful of glass splinters. Irene Selznick did not ask to see me afterwards and Broadway lost an undiscovered talent forever.

I made a decision. I would do something more solid, and it took the form of *American Heritage*, where I started as a secretary and through the usual Horatio Alger process, female variety (volunteering to work three nights a week, Christmas afternoon, and the Fourth of July weekend), became an editor. On April Fools' Day, 1968, I was writing the last chapter of a history of European cathedrals when one of the vice presidents walked in and announced that *American Heritage* was going to publish a paperback book on Robert Kennedy, and starting that afternoon, I would travel with him. So off I flew with my notebook and camera, the magazine's new political reporter. By waving my driver's license in a press-cardy sort of way, I managed to get to the front of the New Jersey hall

☐ 23

where Kennedy was speaking, and by holding the coat-tails (literally) of Carter Burden, a friend who worked for the Senator, situated myself on the press plane. But then how to meet and talk to Senator Kennedy which I had to do if I was going to write a book about him? Pondering this, I was mentally rehearsing an "er-uh, Senator uh-Kennedy, I'm Kristi Witker, and I'm writing a book about you," sort of introduction, when I suddenly felt a tap on my shoulder. "Er-uh, excuse me," a voice said, "my name is uh Robert Kennedy." He turned out to be an accessible candidate.

From then on, traveling on the Kennedy campaign was a relaxing and enormously pleasurable experience. It was during that time that I got to know his press secretary, Frank Mankiewicz; press advisor and California coordinator, Pierre Salinger; and his long-time friend and special traveling advisor, Fred Dutton. It had been an exhilarating and happy time for all of us who followed Bobby Kennedy, and a devastating experience when it ended. Now, 4 years later, it seemed that the Kennedy organization had reassembled. McGovern appeared to represent the same hopes and ideals, and I think a lot of us believed that we'd somehow recapture what we had lost.

I flew to Miami on April 10, checked into the Sheraton Four Ambassadors Hotel, and immediately hitched a ride to our headquarters about eight miles away. Announcing myself to no one in particular, I asked for Gary Hart. "Oh," said a short, blonde girl sitting at one of the few desks, "you must be the statistician we've been waiting for." Well, not exactly, but why not? The campaign was rather unstructured then.

It was harder to put together my key precincts in

Miami than in New Hampshire since Miami had never held a primary before, and therefore had no red book as had New Hampshire, with such useful statistics as who had voted how in the past and who lived where in the present. Not only that, but most of the volunteers at headquarters came from states all over the country, hardly ideal informants on the vagaries of small Florida precincts. Again, the job seemed hopeless. Again, the Florida skies vanished as I sat hunched on a condensed-milk crate phoning strangers in Gainesville asking them to select a nice middle-class ward for me.

One day Frank asked me to meet him by the pool with my most up-to-date demographics. It was the first time I'd been outside and the sunlight was startling. I raised my hand for a second to shield my eyes from the glare—an unfortunate move. One gust of wind and my week's work flew off. And at that moment, along came George McGovern in a bathing suit, swinging a towel. "Hi, Kristi," he said, "how does it look? What percentage do you think we'll get?" I hadn't a clue. My notes were floating down over the pool. But thinking it better to say something and divert him from the key precinct drowning taking place almost under his nose, I answered cheerfully, "Oh, everything looks great. I think we'll get about 14 percent."

McGovern's main objective in Florida was to stop Lindsay, the prime obstacle in his battle for championship of the Left. Working to this end were Queens Democratic leader Matt Troy and some of his supporters who had come down from New York to drive sound trucks relaying messages to the effect, "Now that you've made such a success in New York, Mayor Lindsay, what will you do for the country?" And Dick Tuck had a corps of volunteers waving embarrassing signs at rallies and planting questions at press conferences, where someone could always be found to ask Lindsay any of a myriad of questions about New York's unsolved problems or to ask Muskie why he didn't think a black man was qualified for high office. One planted tormentor noticeably rattled Lindsay in Miami by posing the question, "Where do you stand on our relations with Mexico?"—obviously not a subject on which the Mayor of New York found himself well versed.

The McGovern plan was to "condition" the press; convince them that he had put no real effort into Florida and was therefore, naturally, far behind. To be certain the press got the idea, Tuck typed up some figures supposedly from a secret poll, showing Muskie leading, Lindsay very strong, and McGovern trailing somewhere around one or two percent. The sheet of paper was torn off at the top, then Xeroxed to lend an illicit, stolen look; then Tuck, with it in his pocket, sidled off to find the press. First leaking word that a devastating poll had just been uncovered, he allowed himself to be pressured into releasing it to a young *New York Times* reporter, Christopher Lydon, who begged for the chance to be first with the story.

"Dick Tuck kids around a lot," said Lydon smugly after he had furtively copied down the figures, "but once in a while he comes up with something really important." The ploy worked. The poll *did* condition the press to expect good showings from Muskie and Lindsay and nothing from McGovern. Whatever the Election Day figures, it would look as though the leaders had slipped while McGovern surged.

The night before the primary, there was a big rally at the University of Miami. It was a warm, starry night

26 □

and the crowd went wild, and, for a moment, I thought we *would* get 14%. After McGovern spoke about the War, high prices, and the uneven distribution of wealth, he signed autographs while the crowd continued to cheer. And he suddenly seemed different.

I had met Senator McGovern for the first time the previous summer at a party in his honor in Beverly Hills, where I had gone to write an article for *The New York Times.* It was a low-key party with people standing in tight little knots, and when I arrived, I had realized I was early and knew no one. To pass the time until McGovern arrived, I had attached myself to the hors d'oeuvres table while carrying on a banal conversation with a girl identified solely as "Carrie from the beach." It was only after half an hour of this that I had suddenly discovered that George McGovern *was* there. He was across the room talking to his wife, Eleanor, and a tall, balding man with glasses, who was now heading for the bar, leaving the McGoverns alone. I went over to meet them.

My impression then had been of a very accessible, rather ignored, quiet man and a pretty wife, both of whom actually looked at you when they spoke and listened when you did. We discussed the War, mostly, but I also told McGovern that I thought he should strongly denounce the proposed postal rates which could put so many magazines out of business, and how, if he did that, all the publishers would be for him. He said he agreed, and I left the party, feeling I'd found two people I liked very much.

Now in Florida, McGovern seemed to have a new quality besides his likableness—a kind of star quality. Everyone had said McGovern had no charisma, but they were wrong. Somewhere along the line, Gloria

Steinem had given him advice on clothes, and she had done a great job. McGovern now looked and acted like a winner, and I didn't see how he ever again could be a cocktail party's undiscovered guest.

We didn't win in Florida. We lost rather badly, in fact, coming in last, with six percent of the vote, slightly behind John Lindsay and sixth in a race of six if you exclude Shirley Chisholm and Eugene McCarthy, whose names were on the ballot but who never campaigned in the state. Wallace won with 42 percent of the vote, but somehow that didn't seem to matter, because the press was kind to us. Basically, they boiled it down to: Wallace only won because of the busing issue; Humphrey came in second because of the Jewish vote; Jackson came in third because he rode Wallace's coattails on the busing issue; it was all over for Muskie because he had really slipped and come in fourth; it was terrible for Lindsay because after spending so much money on television he only came in fifth; and it was perfectly O.K. for McGovern because he had done so well in New Hampshire, had spent so little time in Florida, and even so, had managed to surge ahead in the end.

After Florida, Pierre asked if I'd do the same thing in Illinois, which, for the first time, was holding a Presidential preference primary between Muskie and McCarthy. Also, for the first time, there would be balloting for pledged delegates which would give voters a choice of Muskie and McCarthy, plus McGovern. Illinois had always been considered the reliable barometer for "average America," so it was important that we win some delegates. Only it seemed that no one in Illinois

28 ☐

understood how to vote for individual delegates or what it meant. Including me. I was, therefore, immediately given the job of calling myriads of voters and explaining the process to them.

One night after I had thoroughly explained the delegate process to everyone I could reach with a telephone, I went out to suburban Champaign to hear McGovern speak at the University of Illinois. It was the night of Nixon's major speech on busing and 3,000 students jammed the auditorium to hear McGovern. He began by saying he thought everyone should hear the President and he brought a TV set up to the stage with a microphone attached to a loudspeaker. When Nixon finished, McGovern went up to the stage. "What we have just witnessed," he said, "is a collapse of moral and political leadership by the President. He has talked for years about law and order. What he has asked Congress to do now is to defy the courts and defy the Constitution. This course will doubtless be welcomed by many frightened people, but it represents a sneak attack on the Constitution of the United States."

The mood that George McGovern created that night was electric. He believed something strongly and said it. He was the only Democratic contender, it seemed, who could do that, and, once again, I realized that no matter who won in Illinois it was of little consequence. The main Illinois race was, after all, between Muskie and McCarthy, but from now on we would win. We had been saying all along "Wait till Wisconsin." It would happen there. Muskie, with the help of the Press, was on the way down; Humphrey and McCarthy were over; and Lindsay had never begun. There was really no one running against us.

On to Wisconsin, king of the primaries, with 12 candidates on the ballot, only four of them real: Humphrey, still burbling about busing and how, ". . . thank goodness Mr. Nixon has finally come around to some of the things that some of the rest of us have been trying to do"; Muskie, ". . . just beginning to see good, red Polish blood coming to a boil"; Lindsay, trying to convince anyone who would listen that "The Switch is on to Lindsay"; and McGovern with a simple message along the lines of his constantly aired commercial—"If you want lower property taxes, you want George McGovern."

I arrived in Milwaukee late at night and groped down the dark corridors of the small Milwaukee Inn looking for my room. No one was up except one man sitting somewhat rigidly on a chair outside a door several yards away from mine. He was talking up his sleeve and had wires hanging out of his ear. I realized, of course, that McGovern must be in that room and that the Secret Service had finally caught up with us which was good because their arrival meant McGovern was now considered a major Presidential contender, but also bad because the campaign would be less casual now.

I awoke to the silence of a city, and stared out the window at snowswept streets, not the very best day for our schedule which had us driving across the state to the towns of Fond du Lac, Oshkosh, and Neenah with an overnight in Green Bay. But at 7:00 a.m., off we slid on icy press bus wheels for the first stop, a local high school rally. Just after McGovern's speech I was standing at the back of the auditorium talking to Kirby Jones when an aide I'd never seen before rushed up and said something fast to Kirby in muted tones. Kirby turned and quickly followed the man out the door. I felt dizzy and weak. I had heard only one word of the conversation, but it was enough. The word was "killed." With shaking knees, I wobbled outside to find Kirby. "What happened?" I gasped. "The schedule's been killed," he said, "because of the snow." I suddenly realized that the memories of 1968 weren't buried at all; they were right beneath the surface and would never completely go away.

Since we weren't going to Green Bay, McGovern decided to visit some local factories after first stopping at a shoe store to buy a pair of ludicrous-looking galoshes. The first factory was not what you would call a successful stop. We got there at 3:40 p.m., 20 minutes before the end of the shift. There was little sound except the voice of the factory supervisor who stood with McGovern in a small foyer near the front door and below a stairway leading the plant's main hall. The supervisor kept saying "Here he is, George McGovern, the next President of the United States," to anyone interested—only there was no one around except the candidate, 14 reporters and five members of the staff. I felt embarrassed for George McGovern. He looked so vulnerable standing there in a droopy tan raincoat and those floppy, green rubber galoshes. I kept wishing he didn't know me so I could suddenly sweep down the stairs, your basic everyday factory worker, and tell him how much I admired him. And then suddenly the quiet was pierced by a clanging bell and the upper door burst open. It all happened so fast—the shuffling sound of hundreds of feet, blurs of color, a muffled voice calling out, "Here he is, George McGovern, the next . . ." And they were gone. Hundreds of workers had thundered by and he had shaken hands with 20 of them. We all walked back out into the snow. It was a disturbing and lonely experience.

Across the state, figures from a Wisconsin AFL-CIO telephone poll were being leaked to the press, showing McGovern leading with 23%, Humphrey next with 18%, Muskie 13%, Wallace 12%, Jackson 11%, and Lindsay, Chisholm, McCarthy, and Kennedy (who wasn't running), all with 1%.

The big fear in Wisconsin had been one we shared with Muskie—that if Lindsay succeeded in building the kind of power base Bobby Kennedy had had in 1968, it could bring Ted Kennedy into the race. The poll, combined with continued assertions from the press that Lindsay's campaign had suffered a crippling setback in Florida, dissipated that fear.

Meanwhile, the snow was trapping Humphrey across the state in Wausau, forcing him to cancel a busy day of campaigning in four cities; John Lindsay's flight from New York was diverted to Madison, causing him to miss his speech to the Milwaukee Bar Association; and poor Muskie floundered in Sheboygan, unable to fly to a boiling-Polish-blood meeting in Kenosha.

Being a former Lindsay volunteer during his previous mayoral races (I worked from 6 till midnight after my regular job to answer his "gripe line" and explain his positions on various issues), I felt sorry to see him with such a hopelessly low percentage. I couldn't understand it. So, being quite far along in my precinct analyses, I went along with the Lindsay entourage the next day to take pictures and look at his crowds. I caught up with him at noon on Milwaukee's crowded Wisconsin Avenue. It was a cold, blustery day and Lindsay was walking in a slightly hunched-over manner with the collar of his tan military raincoat up and his hands thrust deep in the pockets. A large white button with blue letters pinned to his lapel read "The Switch Is On to Lindsay." "Here he is, the next President of the United States!" a tall windblown boy with a very red nose and similar white button was shouting rather hoarsely. The crowd plunged by, pausing briefly in their lunch hour rush to murmur "Isn't he handsome!" "I touched him," "Mayor who?" He was by far the best-looking, most forceful candidate, but, as a young, bearded photographer next to me said, "He just can't pull his act together in time."

Lindsay's next stop was a garment factory on South Third Street with its rows of sewing machines run by women who seemed to find him attractive but who had obviously been visited by at least three other candidates, judging from the proliferation of campaign stickers on the walls above their machines. Lindsay tried hard to reach them—he told them, "The switch is on," and then successfully turned on a switch—of a sewing machine—and without serious accident, managed to sew a seam on a piece of felt.

Back on the bus, I asked him about the poll. "It's totally unfair," he said. "They call a few people on the phone and then publish any old thing. There's nothing scientific about it. I think the results on Election Day will be the biggest surprise of the political season. There really *is* a switch to Lindsay!"

But there was a weariness in his voice and eyes that I had not detected outside. He leaned up against the seat in front of us and rested his chin on his arms. "A lot of things happen in a campaign that make you very bitter," he said almost inaudibly.

The press bus took us on to the airport where Lindsay

☐ *33*

and his aides were to fly to the northern town of Apple-
ton for one more rally. Except, there was nothing to fly
in. His top aides rushed back and forth through the
quiet charter terminal berating the airline, checking
schedules and jostling each other for the one available
pay phone, but the situation could not be changed.
"The aircraft was delayed for two hours or more for
mechanical reasons." Their schedule was lost, and they
were powerless.

I left the airport, looking back only once to see John
Lindsay, a tall, lonely figure in a tan military raincoat,
hunched over in a plastic lounge chair, his eyes down,
his chin resting on his hands. I was beginning to feel
sorry for all the candidates.

The Wisconsin primary was fun, however, because
most of the events had an unreal, rather childish quality, like a silly game that everyone has to play. We went
to endless bowling alleys, often with Lindsay and Humphrey, their shirtsleeves rolled up, clumsily lobbing
balls on adjoining alleys while McGovern stumbled
through the crowds at the popcorn machines. It always
struck me as an incredible disruption of other people's
lives. Here they were, men and women who worked
hard and were trying to spend a relaxed evening bowling. And what happens? The door bursts open, there's
a blast of television lights, and in comes a candidate lost
in a swirl of newsmen, still photographers, pushy staffers, and hangers-on. Games stop, scores are lost, a non-
bowling candidate suddenly moves in on a stranger's
alley, and, with great bluster, hurls a ball toward the
pins, occasionally striking one.

Then there was the Serbian Fish Fry. Humphrey,
Lindsay, Muskie, and McGovern, heads bobbing and

grinning, all trying to eat fish as though they could taste it, in the casual atmosphere of screaming crowds, intense heat, and blaring TV lights. The fish fry was so crowded that several reporters who came in with Humphrey left with Lindsay, discovering their mistake only after they had roared away to another bowling alley in the wrong press bus.

Our headquarters was a rambling series of dusty, odd-shaped rabbit warrens in a semioccupied building across from the big Pfister Hotel. "Offices" were on two floors, connected by several sets of rickety stairs, and I found myself constantly lost in search of my cubicle which I shared with Pierre, his cigar, and a quiet, pale, 26-year-old called Gene Pokorny. Gene was so unassuming about his role in the campaign and what he actually did that it wasn't until Election Day that I realized he was the Wisconsin campaign manager and the man really responsible for our first victory.

On Election Day morning, I had my first leisurely breakfast—my first breakfast at all actually, with Pierre and his son Marc, who had dropped college temporarily to work on the campaign. Pierre was ebullient. "I'm seeing McGovern in fifteen minutes," he said. "And I'm going to tell him it's time we stopped running a campaign for Senator of South Dakota and started running a campaign for President of the United States!"

Just as I was about to leave the table, Frank Mankiewicz joined us and eased himself into the chair next to me. "I want you to stay on," he said. "I've been talking to the Senator and he thinks we should put you in Washington to run the press office."

I couldn't do it. I was flattered, I said, but I had been offered another job—that I badly wanted—as a TV network reporter, a job which had come through the previous week as a result of my earlier months of job-hunting.

"I'm sure we can work something out," Frank said. "You can do that later. Right now, I really need you—and the Senator needs you, too." I said I couldn't. Frank said think about it. Unfortunately, I began to think about it.

I enjoyed my job on the campaign. Across the telephone lines I talked to friendly, bright people, I was learning about each state, about polling techniques, and about how to run what was becoming a winning campaign. Our only opponent now was Humphrey, Frank said. "At this point to bother attacking Muskie would be like firing torpedoes into the hulk of the Graf Spee."

On Election Night we set up our Situation Room in the Pfister Hotel where Frank, Pierre, Gary, Kirby, Pat Caddell, Pat's assistant Dan Porter, and I would get the first returns. Each of us held a Xeroxed copy, some 40 pages, of my key precincts with blank spaces to fill in the vote. In front of me sat three special telephones on which calls would come in from our poll watchers around the state. When the phone rang, I would call out the page number for the precinct coming in, we would all fill in the numbers, and then Dan would quickly work out percentages on his calculator. As I began calling out figures, which for the first time showed us consistently ahead, the room was strangely quiet.

"This campaign," said Pierre, drawing on his cigar, "is not psychologically prepared for victory." It was a portentious observation.

There was an enormous victory celebration downstairs in the Pfister, only slightly marred by McGovern's secretary, Pat Donovan, who threw a tantrum in her room at the Milwaukee Inn, refusing to come to the victory party even after McGovern sent a limousine back to get her. Our New Hampshire coordinator, Joe Grandmaison, was also moving the story that now that Wisconsin was over, Gary Hart would be fired.

Later that night, Gary, who was still very much on the scene, Kirby, Pat, and I drafted our analysis of the Wisconsin results. With precinct figures to back us, we pointed to McGovern's strength with the farm vote, ethnic groups, Wallace supporters, and particularly blue-collar workers. We talked about the delegates we'd won so far in the primary and nonprimary states, and, for the first time, projected in print that we would have more delegates at the Convention than any other candidate. The following morning, we held a press conference and passed out mimeographed sheets with our analyses and figures. Muskie was finished, the press was saying—a strange conclusion when you remember that he had beaten McGovern by nine percentage points in New Hampshire, three in Florida, and had walked away with the delegates in Illinois, 59 to McGovern's 14. Wisconsin, in fact, was the first primary where, in a contest with McGovern, Muskie had not been clearly the winner.

On the plane back to New York, I told Shirley Mac-Laine about Frank's job offer. "You'd be crazy not to take it," she said. "This campaign is where it's happening. It's going to change politics and the country forever, and you'll be right in there at the White House. You may never have another big chance like this again."

When we arrived at LaGuardia, television crews and a large crowd were on hand to meet a man who had also had his big chance—John Lindsay, who quietly announced that his ill-fated campaign for the Presidency had come to an end.

The rest of that week and the next, I filled in for a man on vacation at WCBS-TV, writing for two evening news shows. It was during this week that Frank telephoned constantly to see if I would take the job with McGovern. I said no. There was a long silence.

"You're making the biggest mistake of your life," he said slowly. "I'm offering you a once-in-a-lifetime opportunity—to be in at the very top of a winning Presidential campaign. You'll be Deputy Press Secretary and you'll be Deputy Press Secretary at the White House. How does that sound? That's a pretty good offer, huh?" I had to admit it was.

With thumping heart and knotted stomach, I finally listened to Frank and turned down the network job. The campaign job *was* a once-in-a-lifetime opportunity, but although I didn't realize it immediately, I had just made the wrong choice.

chapter 3

The Schedule's
Not for Having

Five days later, April 19, I flew to Washington and took a cab to McGovern headquarters in the southeast section of the city. It was a small two-story building crunched between a liquor store and a sandwich shop, identified only by a small blue "McGovern for President" sticker over the door. The door squeaked open, and I stepped into a tiny reception area where a dark-haired girl at a switchboard pointed me toward a narrow corridor at the end of which was Frank's office. He was on the telephone and appeared to be smoking three cigarettes. I put my suitcase down. Frank lit another cigarette, rested the phone in its cradle and looked up. "Hey," he said, leaping to his feet, knocking over a huge stack of mimeographs, and kissing me on the cheek, "Welcome to Washington."

He dangled a set of keys over his desk. "I've found an apartment for you. It belongs to a girl out on the campaign who won't be back for months—so it's yours and it's free." I was delighted. Then he led me into an 8 x 11-foot room filled with three desks and four girls —my new office.

Since one desk was being sat *at* and sat *on* simultaneously and the other two appeared decisively owned, it was difficult to see just where I might fit in. "This is

Kristi," Frank said cheerfully. "She's here from New York to run the press office. I know you girls will make her feel very welcome."

A look of intense pain crossed the nearest girl's face. The other flashed an angelic smile. "Everyone calls me Angel," she purred. Angel was a short, pale, 28-year-old with enormous blue eyes and short fluffy blonde hair. She looked very fragile, and well, angelic. Next to her was Margie, a heavy-set, serious-looking brunette who typed during our introduction, and at "my" desk, Betsey and Bobbie, both in hot pants, who were busy with the consumption of doughnuts and several Cokes.

I called Mother collect in Darien. Being a Republican and a mother, she had naturally strongly urged me to take the network job and was, therefore, not at all pleased to hear I was calling from Washington.

"It'll be a wonderful campaign," I said, trying to sound like I'd made the right decision, "and I have a super apartment on F Street."

"That figures, dear," she said quietly. "F" as in "futile."

At the end of my first day, which I'd spent standing about the miniscule office, sitting down once when Bobbie got up to sharpen a pencil, I set off for F Street. It was in what Washington cheerfully describes as "a high crime area"—a small, deteriorating, four-story house across from a city park and a few doors down from the Department of Welfare. The high intensity street lights (used in high intensity crime areas) illuminated the shadows with an eerie light which made it feel like Halloween. I had one small problem getting into the building, caused by the fact that the front door key did not fit the keyhole. But it was an easily corrected situation. The door wasn't locked.

Inside, I was greeted by an enormous pile of unclaimed mail addressed to various apartments, which made me wonder whether all the occupants had been murdered in their beds. I hoped I wouldn't find out, and quickly groped my way up two flights of stairs, thick in dust and old gum wrappers to the apartment for which the key did fit. Only one small problem there, too. Obviously, I had interrupted some sort of roach reunion and had to wait until all parties dispersed before daring to put down my suitcase. There were no sheets or towels, no soap, and only one light bulb, a nervously flickering little thing that looked as though it wouldn't make it through the night. Quickly, I called a friend and then a cab. None came. I called again. "Listen, lady," said a tired voice across the line. "That's a high crime area you're calling from. Our drivers don't want to go in there."

It was a terrific beginning.

McGovern headquarters suffered an acute lack of space. It also suffered from a lack of air. On the ground floor were five actual offices—a large one for Henry Kimelman, Director of Finance, and his assistants; another for Gary Hart and his assistants; one for Jeff Smith who had something to do with budgets; one for Frank and his assistant; and one for the press. Back of those was a large bull pen with cubicles running along one side for regional coordinators, with signs identifying them as "West," "Eastern," and so on. Then there was a desk for Amanda Smith, the woman who handled women's issues, and another for three people in Scheduling. At the very back of the large room was a mail section with postage meters, a stamp machine, mimeograph and Xerox machines, and a multipurpose bathroom with a movable sign which could be swung to "Male," "Female," or "Empty," depending on the appropriate situation. There were few phones and fewer WATS lines (lines allowing unlimited calls, for a monthly charge).

The room was crammed with folding metal tables, six or eight people at each, typing, stuffing envelopes, collating pages. It buzzed with activity, often punctuated by shrill invective—"That was *my* chair . . . It was, goddamnit, I just got up for a minute . . . O.K. for Chrissakes, take the goddamn chair . . ." "That was *my* typewriter . . . No, goddamn it, I can't use the Olivetti —You know the B, the R and the L are jammed. *You* use it."

I had a slight disadvantage being the fifth person in line for the use of three desks. At first, part of my job involved my watching the CBS Morning News and NBC's *Today* show and reading the New York and Washington papers so I could write a Daily News Digest to wire to McGovern on the road. That meant I couldn't get to the office until after 9, by which time Angel and Margie were firmly rooted to their chairs and Betsey and Bobbie, who were only volunteers but apparently inseparable, had permanently affixed themselves to the third desk, "doing something very important for Angel." Occasionally, I got there first, settled myself in and claimed a desk, a chair, and even a telephone. But then something terrible always happened. I would get a phone call in another office; I would have to make a Xerox copy of a release; or Frank would call me, and when I returned—zap—it was all gone.

Shortly after I started my exciting, demanding job as Deputy Press Secretary, I began to notice a strange

44 □

phenomenon. I started losing things. I don't mean the desk I lost every day. Losing a desk, after all, was understandable. It hadn't vanished. I just wasn't at it. The same with the chair. And the telephone. But one day, having dragged a wobbly typewriter table into the office, I had managed to write up a press release about Senator Ribicoff's endorsement of McGovern. A few minutes later, Frank called through the door that he wanted it. "Sure," I said. I looked at the typewriter table. No release. I retraced my steps—other desks, other phones, the Xerox machine, the refrigerator. The typed sheet was nowhere. "Where's that release?" Frank thundered. "Gulp," I said.

The next day, my problem was worse. I had to write a report based on some figures from the Wisconsin primary. That was simple—they were in a file I kept in the third desk's top drawer. I pulled it out, a manila folder with an index tab lettered in my own hand—"Wisconsin Primary." The file was empty. Now, I had always lost things, but this was getting out of hand. Clearly, I was losing my mind. I thought it better not to mention this to anyone. It could only confirm what they probably already thought. After all, I must have been looking just a bit loony, galloping from office to office just to make a routine phone call, and taking all those messages on the back of my hand.

Fortunately, it was Friday, the day I had to leave for Boston and the next primary. Hopefully, when I returned to Washington, I would be better.

It was cold and rainy when I arrived in Boston, a rather welcome relief from the heat and stuffiness of the Washington office. The campaign group was staying at a modern hotel called the Colonnade, several miles from the center of town and so new that from any distance it looked unfinished.

Checking in was like a reunion—all the familiar faces from earlier primaries dotted the lobby, and everyone waved and called hello. It was a cozy feeling—like being a member of a club.

Before going to our downtown headquarters, I wandered into a small sandwich bar running along the lobby's edge, and joined Bill Dougherty, the boyish, blonde Lieutenant Governor of South Dakota. I had met Bill in Wisconsin and liked him immediately for his friendliness, love of humor, and apparent detachment from everything political. But behind his back country "Hi, how're ya doin, what do ya know?" manner, he was actually one of the shrewdest political pros in the campaign and served as its most effective contact man. Bill seemed to know everyone in any given town from the lowest mill worker to mayor, and he had the particularly refreshing quality of seeming to attach no more importance to one than the other. He carried on his job with endless exuberance but was one of the only people in the campaign who refused to pontificate on the issues. McGovern trusted him absolutely.

While we talked and ate, another old friend whom I hadn't seen in a year, came up, fatherly gray-haired Dick Dougherty (no relation to Bill), former chief of the *Los Angeles Times* New York bureau. Dougherty had taken on the job of Campaign Press Secretary before the New Hampshire primary but, because McGovern didn't listen to him, had quit and returned to New York. Now he was back with a book contract, and I wondered whether he would take over for Kirby Jones, whom

46 ☐

Mankiewicz had appointed in New Hampshire to Dougherty's vacated job. "No," said Dick, "I'm just an advisor, just going along to help where I can."

That night, Bill Dougherty was attending a dinner and auction for McGovern in Rockport, Massachusetts, and asked me to go. It sounded like fun; I immediately accepted and raced off to meet Pat Caddell at headquarters to line up our first precincts. I felt very happy to be back on the road.

The night before the election, I had dinner with Dick Dougherty, newsman Sandy Vanocur, Gary Hart, and a female reporter from Washington on hand to write one of what would become an endless round of newspaper articles about Gary. We went to a huge fish restaurant on the wharf and talked, of course, about the campaign. Since McGovern was the only candidate to make an effort in Massachusetts and because he had just been further bolstered by some well-chosen words from Ethel Kennedy, the mood that night was confident. He would win all 102 Massachusetts delegates, Gary said, one more victory in a battle plan worked out long ago by the top campaign strategists. "We'll lose Pennsylvania tomorrow to Humphrey, but then Muskie will be all washed up. That leaves only Hubert, and we'll beat him in Nebraska, Oregon, California, and New York." His voice trailed off. ". . . though we'll have the nomination wrapped up after California."

The reporter stared at Gary, her expression indicating that she had never before been privy to such astute firsthand political wisdom.

"What do you want to do after the campaign?" Gary asked me in a tone more of politeness than curiosity.

"Go back to reporting," I answered.

He came alive. "What? You wouldn't want to work in the administration?" It was apparently a possibility that had never occurred to him.

"No," I said, "I just want to see George McGovern elected and then go back to real life. And you?"

"I don't know," he said. "I look at the campaign as essentially an exercise. I'm mentally involved, but I'm not passionately involved."

Later, I asked Sandy Vanocur his opinion of Washington, since it was beginning to look as though I'd be based there until November. "You'll hate it," he said simply. "You'll be miserable. Politics destroys everyone in the town. It creeps into every facet of your life, insidiously, like a cancer, until you're consumed by it and can no longer do anything without analyzing the possible political ramifications. Friendships are based on politics, you're invited to dinner parties if you have any political use at that moment, and you're disinvited if you don't." He paused. "But it's a good place to live if you're like me and have problems to work out. It's such a totally dull place that you get a chance for a complete emotional rest."

It sounded awful, and, at that moment, I couldn't imagine that in a few months I too might be needing a complete emotional rest.

When we returned from dinner, there was a birthday party for Shirley MacLaine in the hotel lobby's sandwich bar. It was a verbal "invitation only" event where we all stood around—a few favorite press people, Gary, Gordon Weil, some favorite fat cat donors, and some other staff members, waiting for Shirley, the cake, and the McGoverns. They arrived in that order.

The McGoverns went up to Shirley and hugged her while flash bulbs popped. I noticed that several staff members who had been sitting at a little table with me before McGovern arrived had suddenly jumped to their feet and were very much interested in the birthday cake in front of which Shirley and George just happened to be standing. However, it's hard to examine a cake and get anything but your back in a photograph, so they had now turned ever so casually—rear to cake, faces hanging over the shoulders of birthday child and candidate.

The fact that they were all in the picture and not at the table meant that I was suddenly sitting by myself, feeling somewhat foolish and definitely alone. I was exhausted and would have to work until at least 3 a.m. the following night getting election returns, so why not go to bed? Well—I might be missing something. What? Well—I wasn't sure, but I was among the privileged to be there so maybe I shouldn't leave because SOMETHING might happen, and no one else was leaving. Besides, I hadn't had any cake. So I stayed. But no one cut the cake—it just vanished into the kitchen in the arms of one of the waiters. I walked over to the bar, thinking of chocolate and icing and listened to fragments of conversation, all very much the same—"We'll win Massachusetts; Humphrey will win Pennsylvania which will knock Muskie out; we'll win Nebraska . . ."

Finally, the waiter returned carrying something covered in a sheet. Good God—what had died? Sadly, it was the cake. I suppose, to keep us from fighting over it, the hotel management had seen fit to kill it off in the kitchen. Now it was back, sliced beyond recognition into bite-sized pieces—each piece wrapped tightly in a paper napkin, which could never be removed without serious loss of icing. I wondered if the management had thought it was a wedding. Or, maybe it *was* a wedding and if I went to bed I would really be missing something. Deciding to take my chances, however, I trudged off to my room. I would put the cake under my pillow and maybe it would bring good luck.

On Election Night, we set up our Situation Room in the downtown Statler Hilton Hotel. It was a medium-sized conference room with two banquet tables at either end and a large space with chairs in the center. On the farthest banquet table sat five black, shiny telephones. Milling around the room were columnist Mary McGrory, historian Theodore White, Pat Caddell, Dan Porter, Kirby Jones, Gary Hart, and a very agitated Frank Mankiewicz. And running around the room in tiny circles was an even more agitated young staff worker called Larry Hotel, by virtue of his job handling hotel arrangements.

Frank saw me in the doorway. "The telephones," he said, his voice rising, "No one connected the telephones."

"It was supposed to be done," Larry Hotel said breathlessly. "Really, I handled all these details, and I told the hotel we needed five telephones. They promised to put them in."

"They did," Kirby said, staring at the banquet table. "They put them in the room. But maybe you never mentioned that you wanted them plugged in!" Larry Hotel at the moment was low on humor, high on blood pressure. "I told them, I really told them," he said, panting. "See, I've ordered the tables, and the tablecloths, and the chairs, and the drinks, and the glasses, and ice . . . and . . . and . . ."

"Would somebody get these goddamn phones fixed?" said Frank. "Just do it. Somebody do it."

He did not look happy. Here we were, about to spend the evening with the great historian Teddy White, who would witness our superefficient Situation Room for a segment of *The Making of the President 1972*, and, instead, we have a roomful of gibbering dingbats, five unplugged telephones, and a total news blackout. The situation was, at best, embarrassing.

"Actually, Kristi," said Larry Hotel, brightening for a moment and glancing at Frank and then staring at me, "I thought *you* were going to check that the phones were installed." "Me?" I said, "You know I don't have anything to do with telephones." He smiled. It didn't matter now—Frank had just passed by us.

"Where is some clown to install these things?" asked Gary. "Somewhere," Larry wailed in his helpful manner. "But no one knows where and I can't call the desk because we don't have a telephone and I can't get *down* the elevators because all the elevators are going *up!*"

"Has anyone thought of a pay phone?" asked Teddy White, making the first rational suggestion of the evening. He pulled out a wad of dimes and handed us each two. "Here," he said, "cope."

It seemed an interminable amount of time, but fortunately, the election did not take place before we were able to scrape up the master telephone installer and put him to work in the Situation Room. Everyone calmed down, even Larry Hotel, and the first phone rang. It was Pierre Salinger calling from Paris to report that there seemed to be something wrong with the telephone numbers I had given him. The second one rang, and the third.

"Waltham," I called out, "Ward 3, Precinct 1, middle to upper middle, ethnic, mixed—McGovern 359, Muskie 77, Humphrey 26. South Boston, Ward 6, Precinct 6, Irish, working class—McGovern 165, Muskie 49, Humphrey 31." A cheer went up. It was an indicative beginning. At night's end, McGovern had won in what was considered a landslide with 52% of the vote and all 102 delegates. What was not considered, at least by anyone in the Situation Room, was that, with no real opposition, we had gotten only half the vote. The other half was divided among four candidates not actively in the race—Chisholm, Mills, Humphrey, and Muskie, who had written Massachusetts off so he could devote all his energies to Pennsylvania the same day.

I called our Pennsylvania coordinators. Humphrey had won there with 35%, but we were close behind with 21%, almost neck in neck with Wallace who was just ahead of us, with Muskie trailing behind. The battle plan was right on target. McGovern was thrilled. "Tuesday night," he said, to the ringing cheers of the crowd, "is getting to be the happiest night of the week."

Wednesday morning, we held a press conference and again handed out mimeographed sheets while Gary and Pat answered questions. "McGovern won the votes of those who are dissatisfied with the state of affairs in America today, just as he did in Wisconsin," we said. "He has once again proven that he has a broad base of support which in Massachusetts included working people, suburbanites, students and blacks." Again, as they now did every Wednesday morning, the press took it all down and reprinted it.

"Wednesday," said Kirby, "is getting to be the happiest day of the week."

Back in Washington, the office was just as hot and unventilated as it had been the week before, and every other person had a cold. That day, Margie asked if I'd like to have lunch with her. It was the first time in days that I hadn't eaten a sandwich off my lap and I happily accepted.

We walked down tree-lined First Street and over to Pennsylvania Avenue where a small Italian restaurant perched between a dry cleaner's and a delicatessen. "If I were you," said Margie, "I'd watch out for Angel." "Why?" I asked. "She's one person who seems really nice." "That's how she *seems*," said Margie.

The following morning, Muskie announced his withdrawal, and we all gathered around a television set in the bull pen. It was a sad moment, really. Muskie spoke quietly but more decisively than he had at any time during the campaign. "I have made the decision to withdraw from active participation in the remaining Presidential primaries," he said. "I do not have the money to continue." I wondered whether I did, and made a mental note to remind Marian Pearlman, Henry Kimelman's assistant, that I was owed some back salary and expenses.

I went back to my "office" and settled down on a cardboard box, endside up. It was April 28 and finally beginning to dawn on me that I was never going to have such things in my job as a desk, a chair, or a telephone. It was another contrast to the Kennedy campaign, where there had always been plenty of desks and phones. Not to have had such basics would have smacked of a second-rate operation, intolerable in Kennedy eyes. But apparently this campaign, despite the fact that there was plenty of money available for these things (at least at this time), *preferred* to be second-rate—or at least to look that way.

But what did it matter and why waste time thinking about it? The important thing was to get the job done and my main work was, after all, in the primary states, not at headquarters. However, for the two or three days a week I *was* at headquarters, I needed to function somewhat effectively as a writer of press releases and supplier of schedule information to the press. This was a bit harder to accomplish than one might think.

McGovern's schedule, quite logically, originated out of an office in the bull pen called Scheduling, run by a tall, lank-haired individual called Steve Robbins. The press office could only get the schedule through Robbins; so, the thing to do, of course, was to ask him.

So I asked him for the Saturday schedule. Robbins looked up with the expression of a man carrying six parcels and a steamer trunk who has just been asked if he can spare a match. "Ohio," he said curtly. I had already guessed that. I cleared my throat. "Could you tell me where in Ohio?" I asked. "The press wants to know." He sighed. I could see I was boring him. "Maybe you could just show it to me," I suggested. "I'll write it down." Robbins sighed louder. "The Senator's leaving Cleveland and going to Cincinnati and Toledo. Then there's a dinner in Toledo and two speeches and he'll overnight in Cleveland," he said in a monotone. That was helpful but not quite helpful enough. Reporters have a way of asking these tiresome details such as what *time* might the Senator be in Cincinnati, *where* is the speech, *how* is he getting from Toledo to Cleveland, *what* hotel is he staying at, is there space on the plane, and other such information concerning their joining the trip. "Could I have just a few more details?" I asked, shifting my feet nervously.

"JESUS CHRIST," he bellowed. "I DON'T KNOW, I DON'T KNOW. I don't have the goddamn schedule. And I am busy, REALLY BUSY. FOR CHRISSAKES,

54 □

I'M BUSY." I backed away. The room vibrated from the explosion and my heart was pounding, but I realized suddenly that this outburst was not an uncommon occurrence. Robbins' assistant, Lizzie, just two feet away, hadn't once looked up from her desk.

I crept back to my cardboard box feeling a trifle rejected. The phone on Bobbie's desk rang. I picked it up. "Hi," said a voice, "This is Frank Starr from the *Chicago Tribune*. "Could you tell me McGovern's schedule for Saturday?"

"Uh," I said. "He's going to Cincinnati and Toledo, and there's a dinner in Toledo and two speeches, and he'll overnight in Cleveland." Angel was watching me. Hang up, I prayed, Mr. Starr, please hang up.

"Could you give me a few more details?" asked Starr.

"Uh, well—," I said.

Angel picked up her phone and punched my line. "Hi, Frank," she purred into her end. "This is Angel. The schedule, yes, of course. At 3:30 he leaves Burke Lakefront Airport at 1501 North Marginal Road in Cleveland and arrives at Lunken Field, Cincinnati at 4:45; then, there's a walking tour of Leggett and Steffen Streets in Lincoln Heights at 5:15, and . . ." It went on for 10 minutes with all the details of a moon mission. When she hung up, I realized that someone called Starr now thought I was a blithering fool and that he was, of course, right.

"I couldn't get the schedule from Steve," I said weakly. "He said he didn't have it." Angel looked at me with steely eyes and gave a long sigh. This seemed to be a day for a lot of sighing at headquarters.

Margie took me aside. "The problem is," she said, "that you don't have any power base. You're not established as someone really important here because you're gone most of the time and you don't have anyone high up protecting you. If you don't have a power base, you can't do favors for anyone and if you can't do favors for them, they don't need you."

"What do I have to do for Steve Robbins to get the lousy schedule?" I asked.

"Oh, if you know some tidbit of information from the press office or Frank, give it to him exclusively, or be sure he knows you've said a good word about him to Gary. You see, he thinks, why should he give you the schedule? It sort of diminishes his power—it means he no longer has something you can't get. By denying you, he has control, and you're groveling and looking like an idiot. He has the schedule, you don't, and he wins and you lose all around."

She was right; but sadly, it was knowledge I couldn't use. Traveling as much as I did, I realized I could never get myself one of those power bases. I had also begun to realize how really firmly entrenched the McGovern staff was. It was as though everyone had dug his foxhole during the spring thaw and now, when the ground was frozen, I was out there trying to chip at it with a plastic fork.

Unlike other political campaigns I had seen, this one was Big Business. Most political campaigns are assembled quickly in a matter of a few weeks or months so that no one has time to burrow in before he's caught up in the feverish pace of an election campaign. But McGovern had announced his candidacy almost a year and a half before. His staff was already a corporate structure—each member with a niche, an office, and that treasured power base. The atmosphere was also quite like that of a summer colony: the Establishment versus the newcomers. To have been involved in the campaign from the beginning rated you far higher than having just joined; having come in before New Hampshire was at least several points higher than having joined later.

The younger but higher up McGovern staffers walked around dragging a heavy mantle of prestige, but it was *future* prestige. Gary Hart wasn't regarded as a 34-year-old lawyer from Denver. He was already, in the month of April, Special Assistant to the President; Frank Mankiewicz was Attorney General; Gordon Weil, Secretary of the Treasury; Rick Stearns, Ambassador to the UN. None of them announced their own ambitions, however. It was simply agreed on by others.

I was beginning to know what I was going to be and it wasn't Deputy Press Secretary as Frank had promised. If I could pull together one of those power bases in time, maybe I'd be chosen to look after Atticus, Mary McGovern's dog.

Since I had arrived in Washington and discovered Frank's choice apartment to be less than habitable, I had been sleeping on a friend's sofa bed. It now occurred to me that, since I would never have a desk, it was important for my sense of well-being to make a genuine effort to at least have a home. So I exchanged my waning funds at the local store for a family sized can of Raid, two mops, a broom, a dustpan, Brillo, soap, sheets, pillow cases, towels, and six sponges.

I felt quite hopeful as I scoured, sprayed and swept the roaches out of my life. I was spending my first night in my new apartment. Everything would work out all right.

chapter 4

Winning by Default

Ohio had been a late scheduled primary. It had first been agreed that since Ohio was strong Humphrey territory, McGovern shouldn't enter and risk a loss. Then it was decided that a no-show in the first industrial Midwest primary might look like an admission of low blue-collar support. So we entered.

Arriving at the Neil House Motor Inn in downtown Columbus at midnight, I was sure we'd made a mistake. McGovern and most of the press were in Cleveland and would not arrive at the Neil House for several days. In the meantime, the hotel was hardly empty; it had 1,000 Elks in residence for a three-day convention.

I put down my suitcase and lined up at the Registration Desk. An Elk lurched toward me. "Why are you for that Commie, girlie?" he shouted, stumbling over my suitcase and spilling something that smelled like bourbon on my foot. I glanced around for the Communist I presumed to be at my elbow. But the only thing there was a pair of Elks.

"What Commie?" I asked.

"That one," the three of them said in unison, pointing at my McGovern button, "the one with the big giveaways."

It wasn't the hour for a political argument. I hadn't

☐ 59

had the sense to take the dinner flight, and I hadn't yet been assigned my room. "I just think he's the best candidate," I said somewhat self-righteously.

"Ah, come on, Ralph," said Mrs. Elk, pulling her husband's blue seersucker jacket. "Don't waste your time talking to an uneducated hippie kid."

Columbus was an open, flat, cheerful city and headquarters was the same. We had two floors of actual offices, and everyone working there seemed agreeable, to the point of being downright friendly. There, for the first time, I met Bob McAlister, the blonde Ohio State Chairman, and Harold Himmelman, young, curly haired National Field Organizer, who would, after the Ohio primary, become Gary Hart's Washington assistant. Pat Caddell met me at headquarters along with Barbara Runyon, a helpful volunteer, and once again, we went to work on precincts.

On Election Day as I started collating my finished sheets, I heard someone announce a phone call to a girl across the room. It was for Judy, the girl in whose apartment I had now taken up residence in Washington. She looked friendly and, when she hung up, I jumped up and went over. "Hi," I said, "I'm so glad to meet you. I'm the girl who's living in your apartment."

There was a stricken expression superimposed on total silence.

"You're *what?*" she said. Even through long hair, I perceived her ears going back. Fur bristled. "You're living in my apartment?" The voice went up. "How did you get into my apartment?"

I was getting a trapped burglar sensation. All the typewriters in the room fell silent. "Frank gave it to me," I mumbled, sensing the stares of a roomful of people who had suddenly discovered a lock picker in their midst.

"Frank Mankiewicz!" the voice went up to its highest pitch. "How dare he give you the keys to my apartment! I never told him he could do that. That's incredible . . . the nerve . . . I can't believe it." She stopped and glared at me. "HONESTLY!" she said, and stormed down the stairs.

And it had been such a nice day. Typewriters started up again, conversations resumed and a couple of people even spoke to me, but now I wondered what they *thought*.

In the afternoon, I made up a list of people to work later that night in Room 528, the Situation Room. From somewhere, word had come down to keep the list as small as possible, that people had been coming in that shouldn't be in, and that the important thing was to keep them OUT. Later, when I arrived at the door, a muscled, crewcut man with the eyes of a Doberman pinscher greeted me. "Name?" he said, stepping forward and successfully blocking my way. "Witker," I said with supreme confidence. "Not on the list." He smiled for the first time. "Only those on the list allowed in this room." "That's *my* list," I wailed. "I made it this afternoon." "Well, you're not on it—so I'll have to ask you to leave."

The whole thing was getting away from me. "Look," I said, my hurt feelings and confusion finally turning to fury, "I don't know who you are or who asked you to stand here, but that's my list in your hand and the room

I'm working in that you're blocking, so if you don't mind moving . . ."

Surprisingly, he moved. "I'll see," he looked at the list, "Mr. Man-ki-a-witz about this!"

The 12 of us privileged to work in the room settled down to get the returns, and the first ones were encouraging: Lorain, Ward 8, precinct D, skilled blue-collar workers, considered "highly alienated group"—Humphrey 38, McGovern 65; Akron, Ward 2, Precinct B, blue-collar rubber workers—Humphrey 43, McGovern 56. They came in sporadically, but there was nothing from Cleveland.

The telephone rang, and Harold Himmelman lunged at it. There was a long silence. "What?" he said. "That's impossible. Listen to this, Frank—from Cleveland—Humphrey 109, McGovern 1!" He turned back to the phone. "We're sure as hell gonna put some people in jail for this. It's just too goddamn obvious."

There was a sudden flurry at the door. The crewcut Doberman had been standing watch and had finally caught an intruder. He emitted a throaty growl. "You're not on the list," he snarled. I looked up. The Doberman looked at me, now apparently approving my presence because apparently Mr. Man-ki-a-witz had. "Do you know this man?" he asked threateningly.

"Yes," I said, quite sure of myself at last. "You can let him in, he's Gary Hart."

The television set sputtered and on came Walter Cronkite with the midnight election news. Humphrey had beaten Wallace in Indiana, 46% to 41%, he announced sleepily, and with 17% of the Ohio vote in, Humphrey was leading 41% to 36% over McGovern.

More noise at the door. The Doberman had another one, this time Judy, the girl with the apartment. I waved her in. She probably wants to apologize, I thought.

Judy came over to the sofa where I was sitting with two telephones in my hand, both spouting negative returns. "I want you out of the apartment tomorrow," she said quickly. "I've rented it."

I looked over at Frank, but he was deep in conversation with Bob McAlister. "Could I have one more day?" I asked weakly, "I'll be up all night and I have to fly back to the office tomorrow. I don't know when I'll be able to pack and find another place to stay."

"Sorry," she said, "it's all arranged for tomorrow," and, with that, she backed hurriedly out of the room.

The telephone rang again. I picked it up numbly. "We've got another Cleveland precinct," said a voice, "black middle class—Humphrey 127, McGovern 3."

"I think," said Frank, "it's time to start getting some judges out of bed." He reached for a telephone. At 5 a.m., the ballot count in Cincinnati stopped, not to be resumed for 12 hours. Frank was now in his eighth hour of almost uninterrupted phone calls. "I don't want to insult your city," he was saying to someone (Secretary of State Brown?), "but I've seen better election results in Paraguay!"

Another night in the Situation Room was over.

The press conference Wednesday morning took place on schedule, but it wasn't the lighthearted "Frank and Gary Show" we were used to. Humphrey had won, with 41% to our 40%, but Frank dismissed his narrow victory. "This election," he said, "compares to the 1969 election of Velasia Ibarra in Equador, which, next to South Vietnam, was perhaps the most flagrantly crooked election in the history of the Democratic process."

There was one thing about returning to the Washington office—nothing had changed. Robbins maintained his vicelike grip on the schedule, Angel always looked like an angel, and everyone still looked nervously over his or her shoulder when entering or leaving a room. This time, however, there was one difference. My cardboard box was gone, most probably thrown out by some careless soul not realizing that, for a brief instant, he had held an entire office in his hands.

On the positive side, however, I was at least no longer losing things, perhaps because I now literally affixed items of importance to my person, like mittens on a string through a coat sleeve.

First, I went to look for my mail and see Marian Pearlman whom I hoped would now have my expense check ready for the Massachusetts and Ohio primaries. She didn't but, with a semivacant stare, promised to have it when I returned from the next primary—in Nebraska. My mail brought a telegram with a simple little request from New York millionaire-philanthropist Stewart Mott. "Will you agree to make donations to George McGovern for the next six months?" it read, "$100 on May first, plus $100 monthly during the next five months. The McGovern candidacy deserves every dollar you can afford to give."

At 7 p.m. that first evening back, I gathered up my suitcase and prepared to go to my lost apartment and pack. "Oh—uh—you leaving now?" asked Bobbie, looking at her watch with an expression that implied it said 12 Noon. "I have to move out of the apartment," I told her apologetically. "Oh, well—I'll be here several more hours," she sighed with a weariness of tone and slumpingness of back that riddled me with guilt although she had arrived that day at 2 p.m. I was starting to get

64 ☐

caught up in the campaign's "artificial work ethic."

Normally, I left the office at 9: often, because I needed some time to find a place to sleep that night; sometimes, because I was tired from crouching or standing all day; and occasionally, because some good-hearted soul had offered to provide me with a meal. Whatever the reason, a 9 o'clock departure was always met with cold stares or sighs. This had bothered me until one evening when I had returned to the office for my umbrella and had found, to my astonishment, that the room which just 10 minutes before had pulsated with the energies of late-staying altruists, was now completely empty and dark.

The artificial work ethic precedent had apparently been set early in the campaign by George Cunningham, a long-time aide in McGovern's Senate office, whose main achievement, before signing up with McGovern when he ran for Congress in 1956, had been to serve as President of the South Dakota Young Democrats. According to some of the first campaign recruits, Cunningham had an unusual sleeping pattern, arising at 4:30 a.m. and getting to the Senate office at 6, whence he would promptly telephone the campaign office. This rather unproductive action would later justify his informing McGovern that "when I telephoned the campaign office this morning, no one was in yet." "It happened almost every day," said Ed O'Donnell, a 23-year-old student coordinator, "Gary was always calling us in and saying that he'd heard we were all coming in too late or leaving too early. It wasted an awful lot of time."

There were genuine early and late workers, of course, a special night staff, mostly students, who came in at 6 p.m. and worked until midnight, as well as a hard core of dedicated regular staffers. More often, however, lateness of stay was in direct reverse proportion to hardness of work. The important thing was to look as though you were working—to have your physical presence in a chair.

Political campaigns naturally attract a sizable number of hangers-on, people who find excitement and an instant sense of belonging they have missed in their regular lives. Campaigns are also largely made up of people who just happened to be available for work at the time the staff was being organized. And often, they just happened to be available because no other employer wanted them. For these people, the campaign becomes their entire life. They work until 2 a.m. simply for want of other plans.

Unfortunately, it doesn't stop there. If it did, campaigns would be infused with a bonus of many extra man (or woman) hours. Instead, these extra hours are often spent unproductively. Trying to look busy when not is a much more exhausting endeavor than actually working and results in a time-consuming energy waste which can carry over to the next day, impairing productivity in an ever-increasing cycle. In addition, the jealousy those individuals feel toward anyone who appears to have another life somewhere outside the stuffy confines of headquarters is often so intense as to cut off their productivity for good.

Important lesson to learn: When joining a campaign, either genuinely work until midnight, moving about from time to time for maximum exposure, or having finished your actual work, creep out a back entrance, being sure to leave some telltale piece of work on your desk, implying an intended return. Tell yourself eleven times a day—it's not how things are that counts, it's how they *seem.*

I guess it seemed I was leaving early that night, but I walked boldly toward the door, stopping briefly to phone my only friend in town to announce my unexpected reappearance. She was not exactly elated, but did agree to house me once more and even to collect me and my luggage in her car.

It seemed only right to leave Judy's apartment just as I'd found it, but it was difficult. Why, I asked myself, had I spent money on cleaning equipment and carted out all that dirt when I now could have sprinkled it around for the new tenant? I wondered whether there might be a store in Washington open till 10 that supplied cockroaches by the yard. But there was nothing in the Yellow Pages under roaches, however, except an ad for Raid, which reminded me that it, the mops, pails, sheets, sponges, and towels might make a lovely house present for my friend, or several house presents for several friends if my moving pattern for the spring continued.

With two suitcases, armloads of hardware, and a feeling of extreme rootlessness, I once again wandered off into the Washington dusk.

The campaign had left for Nebraska somewhat on the defensive. This was the state, McGovern said, where we would have to meet the threat of the triple A's (amnesty, abortion, and acid) head-on. In Michigan, Jackson had leveled charges that McGovern was a big supporter of all three but, at that time, rather than stir up the issue further, we had chosen to ignore it, a decision the staff thought had cost us that primary. Now he had swept through Nebraska with the same charges and the issue could no longer be ignored. Anti-McGovern pamphlets were everywhere in the state, portraying him as a radical of sinister dimensions.

In Omaha, I met Warren Weaver of *The New York Times*, who mentioned that his paper had no photographer scheduled for McGovern's train ride across Nebraska. He asked if I could do it. Not having been reimbursed for expenses for the last 2 months, I jumped at the offer.

We got off to a slightly late start the next morning because McGovern was taping a special TV film to be shown statewide on Sunday night, 2 days before the primary. Our media expert, Charles Guggenheim, had been snatched from a Caribbean vacation to put it together—a once-and-for-all disclaimer that McGovern favored abortion on demand, amnesty for everyone, and marijuana for all.

In a cold rain, but a holiday mood, we boarded our train. At the very back of the train, there was a covered platform, hung with a blue sign—"President McGovern—'72." The skies cleared; the air warmed; the crowds cheered.

While I was photographing McGovern, one of the aides pulled me aside. "Why are you taking pictures?" he asked. "Everyone on the staff wants to know." I told him about *The Times*. "But why?" he asked, wrinkling his brow. "No one understands." I was getting another paranoia attack, like an about-to-be-discovered CIA agent. Who were all these "everyones" and "no ones"? It made me nervous to think so many pairs of eyes were occupied with my temporary photographic career. There must be something else for them to do, such as maybe run the campaign.

I began to realize, however, that besides being made

up of available people, political campaigns also consist of people who do only one thing. They have titles, and they usually do something the title suggests. That way, they can pinpoint one another. Each knows the other's capabilities and, therefore, his potential threat. If you're doing several unrelated jobs, you naturally pose a greater threat than if you're doing one labeled job. You can no longer be as easily defined, and not knowing exactly what you do makes it considerably harder to put you down for doing it badly.

The Nebraska campaign ended on Monday, May 8, with Nixon's televised announcement of the mining of Haiphong Harbor. The Senator and most of the staff we were told, would return immediately to Washington. Kirby and I would stay and do Election Night alone. Almost all of us felt as frightened as we had in 1962 when President Kennedy had announced the presence of Russian missiles in Cuba, but, by the next morning, the small staff remaining in Omaha felt happier. In fact, they said, "Last night will be remembered as the turning point in the campaign. Nixon blew it. Now more people will be frightened. They'll see his Vietnamization plan has flopped or he wouldn't be so desperate that he had to mine the harbor." As it turned out, Nixon's speech *was* a turning point, but in the opposite direction.

Election Night went smoothly. Returns flowed in, telephones rang, and after 2 hours' sleep Kirby and I left Omaha on the 6:20 a.m. flight to St. Louis, and then on to Washington for the press conference giving out our key precinct figures and analyses. We had beaten Humphrey 42% to 35% and had added farmers to McGovern's broadening coalition of students, blue-collar workers, and suburbanites.

Holding a press conference in our tiny headquarters was not a happy experience. Tables had to be disassembled, desks moved, all chairs given to the press. With just the usual staff in the room, the heat and stuffiness were suffocating. Add 40 or 50 reporters and three or four TV lights, and the situation became overwhelming. That morning seven people staggered out for air.

When it was over, I expressed my hope to Frank that, after the nomination, we would move to larger quarters somewhere, that maybe the interests of our People's Campaign would be better served by not causing the people to faint.

"But you've missed the whole point," he said. "This tiny, tacky headquarters is our *image*, and our underdog image is the most important thing we've got. To move out of here would ruin it. We're gonna stay right here through November 7." My heart fell.

The next day, possibly to appease Amanda Smith, who was Women's Rights Coordinator, and having a hard time finding many in this particular campaign, Frank agreed to put out some press releases pointing out how McGovern liked women so much he was giving them nifty jobs in his campaign. I would be the first. The release was mimeographed and ready to go out to our list of newspapers and wire services on Friday, May 12, the day I left for the Michigan primary.

"Frank Mankiewicz, National Political Director of the McGovern for President campaign," it began, "announced today that Kristi Witker has joined the national staff as Deputy Press Secretary." And it went on for seven lines to elaborate my past accomplishments. I thought it was quite beautiful and Amanda Smith was pleased. Immediately, I sent one off to Mother, and boarded the plane for Detroit feeling happy.

The Michigan headquarters was not a happy shop. On arrival, Frank had told me to see Laird Harris, Political Director of the Michigan campaign, who turned out to be young, good-looking, and well-informed, and who even offered me the volunteer services of a girl called Leisa Padgett who had finished her work in the office as Assistant Scheduler. Everything had been functioning fine, said Leisa, until some special staff people had come in from Washington and had taken over, by-passing the original Michigan workers, and taking credit for work done before they had even arrived. "We call them the trippers," she said, "because of the ego trips they're on."

Joe Grandmaison, who had coordinated the New Hampshire campaign and whom I'd seen briefly in Massachusetts and Ohio, was one of the importees to the Michigan office. He appeared on a Michigan staff list as "Special staff in charge of political operations." I had always liked Joe. He was a short, fat man with a cherubic face supported by several chins, who had previously worked for the Consolidated Food Company, and whom Hunter Thompson in *Rolling Stone* magazine had rather unflatteringly described as "a cross between a state trooper and a used car salesman." But he was a hard worker and had a voice loud enough to be heard for several blocks when he wanted something done. "He's O. K.," I said, "just try to stay out of his way."

There was not much to do in Detroit except work, so we did. By Sunday morning, 2 days before the primary, we were as far as we could go without further information coming Monday, so I decided to spend the afternoon photographing McGovern as he campaigned around the state.

"You can't," said Grandmaison, pricking up his ears in the direction my conversation with Leisa. "The plane's full." O. K., I thought, I'll take some pictures at a black church where he was scheduled to stop enroute to the airport.

Kirby was in the crowd at the church. "I guess the plane's full," I said. "Maybe," he answered, "but the list's so screwed up I can't tell. Come out to the airport if you want, and take a chance." I did and the chance was good. Two reservationless English journalists and I got on at the last minute and hopped around Michigan for 4 hours of speeches and rallies at Lansing, Saginaw, and Grand Rapids. Crowds were enthusiastic, and the chance for pictures good.

Also, somewhere between Saginaw and Grand Rapids a very important thing happened. Gordon Weil gave me a Staff pin. It was a small, white, much-coveted square that said simply "Staff," but it was considerably better-looking than the cardboard badges most people had, that hung from clumsy jagged-tooth clips or knotted dirty strings. This one was smaller and very classy. It infused me with a sense of belonging that, by now, I would have had trouble achieving without some external symbol.

I was actually very lucky to get one. Staff pins were reserved for those who traveled and were considered "close" to the Senator. However, it was often hard to discern just who was really close and who was just a little close and therefore only entitled to cardboard credentials. How often did you have to have the Senator's ear to be close? Were two ears better than one? No one was quite sure, the result being a constant surge of staffers practically crawling down McGovern's neck.

I attached my new pin to my sweater with the greatest care and continued to photograph McGovern shaking hands with excited students and ladies in hair curlers. It was a pleasant afternoon.

At midnight, the telephone rang in my room. It was Pat Caddell from California. "What on earth is going on?" he asked. "Grandmaison called me, and he's hysterical. Said you'd taken all his volunteers away from their regular work and made them work for you while you went flying around the state with McGovern."

What volunteers? What work? I couldn't believe it. Tiredly, I explained to Pat what had actually happened. "What should I do?" I asked.

"Don't do anything until I get there tomorrow," he said. "Just keep a low profile." As it turned out, it was the wrong advice.

On Monday morning, just to be sure I wasn't losing my mind, I checked with Leisa to see if she'd been working for me while I was "flying around." "Hell, no," she said, "I didn't even come into the office."

Others, however, clarified the episode. It seemed that a *Life* magazine reporter, Bill McWhirter, and his photographer had been traveling with McGovern for several days doing research for an upcoming article on McGovern's staff. They were both along on Sunday and, apparently, several staff members who would not normally have gone on that trip were exceptionally anxious to do so in order to have their presence noted; hopefully to wangle their way in front of the camera and into the article.

Besides that, the normal state of campaign Planeophobia was beginning to develop. There is a certain time in every traveling political campaign—and this was it—when The Plane takes over for The Phallus. The Plane becomes the nerve center, a flying capsule of raw, isolated, sexual Importance. To be on The Plane is to be loved, cared for, needed. To be anywhere else when The Plane is flying is to have missed out hopelessly, to have, in effect, lost your masculinity.

I did not go along, needless to say, to assert my masculinity, but I did enjoy the coziness of life on board. It was like being a child again with everything done for you and no responsibility of your own. You were given a printed schedule telling you what you were about to see and hear; you were handed another sheet telling you what you *had* seen and heard; you were fed, constantly counted, and herded on and off buses and The Plane like children on an outing to the Natural History Museum. It was, perhaps, an acquired taste, but it had definite appeal.

My problem was that I had believed Grandmaison when he said the plane was full. When it wasn't, I simply thought he'd made a mistake—I never considered any other motives behind the words. I was learning—but slowly. Oh, well, I thought, he'll forget it.

And it was easy to forget it and almost everything else because the news that afternoon obscured it all. Wallace had been shot, perhaps fatally, while campaigning in Maryland. Work ceased and everyone at the storefront sat and stared in disbelief at the television screen. We had heard all the words before—"The bullet passed through . . . Doctors are now operating on . . . The hospital will release another bulletin at . . ." It all seemed futile. McGovern, who was campaigning in a city across the state would return immediately to Washington. As far as most of us were concerned, the Michigan campaign was over.

I did the election night returns with Leisa and Gary Hart, with Hunter Thompson looking on. Strangely, the returns came in faster and more completely than at any other time in the campaign. Wallace led, but we were well ahead of Humphrey; Battle Creek, Precinct 10, blue-collar—Wallace 313, McGovern 120, Humphrey 41; Detroit, CD 16, Precinct 30, middle-aged, white, working class—Wallace 219, McGovern 111, Humphrey 37. And so it went until 50 precincts came in.

At 2 a.m., I was sitting in the Situation Room with Peggy Wheeler, an assistant on the State Office Staff, trying to move my fingers over the typewriter keys in a way that would produce numbers on a page to tele-type to the Washington office. Suddenly, a very weary-looking AP photographer stumbled in. "Quick," he said, "I need a picture of something to do with the campaign for the paper tomorrow." He took the only one he could get, but it typified a campaign anywhere —two tired, limp-haired girls under a McGovern banner, Peggy with a glazed expression staring at sheets of figures, me with the telephone cord clenched between my teeth. It ran the next day. Horrors, I thought when I saw it, if they already think the McGovern campaign is run by incompetent speed freaks, this will clinch it.

Wallace had won with 51% of the vote to our 27% and Humphrey's 16%. Three hours later, I teletyped the figures to Frank and again raced for the plane. We held our press conference in Washington that after-noon at 3 o'clock. "Yesterday's Presidential primary election in Michigan showed that Senator George McGovern could take on Senator Hubert Humphrey on Mr. Humphrey's own terms on his own turf and win," we said. Again, the press crushed into headquarters, the TV lights came on, people gasped for air. Another Wednesday, another victory, even though we hadn't won. In fact, though no one seemed to notice, we had now lost Illinois, Ohio, and Michigan—our only three industrial Midwest primaries.

For the first time, it was beginning to occur to me that maybe we were fooling ourselves. We were so wrapped up in semantics about how well we were doing with this and that income or ethnic group that we had come to believe our own advertising. The unspoken feeling seemed to be that if you called defeats victories often enough and convinced enough newspapers of your massive blue-collar support, it would all come true. Perhaps, but if you begin to believe your own illusions, you no longer see the situation as it really is, and not seeing it, you can never correct or improve it.

In Ohio, Frank had outlined our overall campaign strategy. Getting the nomination was the hard part, he said, but after that, beating Richard Nixon would be a snap. All we had to do was put together a massive voter registration drive and media effort in about ten states: New York, California, Michigan, Pennsylvania, New Jersey, Ohio, Texas, Massachusetts, Illinois and Indiana, for instance, and forget the rest of the country. Just concentrate on the states with the big electoral votes. At the time, I must have thought this sounded like a pretty sage idea or I wouldn't later have tried to pass it off as my own. Tired of hearing various self-appointed experts tell me I didn't know anything about politics, I determined to impress upon them my newly acquired wisdom. So the next time I found myself in a political discussion, I dropped my 10-states plan. "Wow," said the man I was talking to, "you sure don't know anything about politics!"

We needed some broader vision, but it wasn't

around. McGovern was stuck with the people who had put him where he was. Many of them had always had unrealistic and inflexible notions about politics, but now, unfortunately for McGovern, they were no longer offstage. They were the center of the show.

And just as they were coming up, the campaign on its own was going down. We were being deprived of our most important issue, the War. Nixon appeared to be getting away with the mining of Haiphong Harbor and convincing Americans that his get-tough policy had worked. Newspapers carried stories of protests, but they were countered by Nixon spokesmen such as Kansas Senator Robert Dole. "The news media," he said, "is presenting a false picture of a deeply divided America in a nervous crisis, rather than the true picture of a largely unified America standing firmly behind the resolute but carefully planned and calmly decided actions of its President." Had we so completely misjudged the mood of the country? Apparently. Just this morning (Wednesday, May 17) a big ad had appeared in *The New York Times* signed by ten citizens supporting the mining. "Who can you believe," the ad asked, *"The New York Times* or the American people?"* (It later turned out that Nixon operative, Charles Colson, had written the ad, paid for by Nixon campaign funds, but, of course, we didn't know that then.) At the same time, Ron Zeigler was claiming that letters, telephone calls, and telegrams sent to the White House were running 5 or 6 to 1 in support of the President (later we found out the Republicans had sent the telegrams to themselves), and an outfit called Opinion Research Corporation published results of a telephone poll which showed that three out of four Americans were behind Nixon. It all sounded very fishy.

Since the War had been the most important issue of McGovern's campaign, it was essential now that we reassess the country's mood, do our own poll, and fight what certainly gave the appearance of managed news coming from the Administration. It was also important, now that Wallace was out of the race, to reassess the meaning of his vote. But, of course, we didn't reassess anything because the staff experts had already made up their minds. We kept saying the War was our best issue and that the McGovern and Wallace phenomenons were the same. Wallace attracted the "alienated" voter. So did we. Therefore, with Wallace out of the race, that vote would go to us. No one considered the fact that there might be different kinds of alienation, and that, quite often, what alienated the Wallace voter was George McGovern.

But a relatively happy afternoon stretched ahead of me, and I didn't want to spoil it worrying. Bobbie had gone to the dentist that day and Angel was sick, a delightful coincidence which provided me with a desk and privacy at once. I leaned back in Angel's chair and stretched my legs. Clunk. My bare toe recoiled in pain into my sandal. I had struck the waste basket. That was some heavy wastebasket. I pulled it out and stared down at the contents with disbelief and galloping paranoia. There, stacked almost lovingly, partially concealed under three Kleenexes, a doughnut wrapper, and a styrofoam cup with coffee drooling out of it, were several hundred press releases. Even through the coffee, I could unfortunately make out some of the words. "Frank Mankiewicz, National Political Director of the McGovern for President campaign, announced today that Kristi Witker had joined the national staff . . ." I was not feeling loved.

Some money would make me feel better, I thought, and I knew just who had some—dashing Henry Kimelman, the Finance Director. I marched in to see him, clutching my several unpaid expense accounts. "Jeff Smith's handling that," he said, waving vaguely toward the door.

Jeff Smith had never heard of me or my expense accounts. "See Marian Pearlman," he suggested. And Marian said she knew she'd promised this week but she had really meant next.

I had no money for Oregon and, as I was leaving the next day, I went next door to the liquor store to see if they would cash a personal New York check. The man at the counter had never laid eyes on me but had no interest at all in seeing my identification. "You're working for the McGovern campaign," he said, "That's good enough for me. Their credit's great!"

In Oregon, as in Massachusetts, we campaigned against ghosts—Muskie, McCarthy, Jackson, and Lindsay, all of whom had dropped out; Mink, Mills, and Chisholm, who hadn't been seen for months; Ted Kennedy, who wasn't running; Wallace, who was now in the hospital and had never come to the state; and Humphrey, who long ago had announced his decision to skip Oregon in favor of California. Once again, McGovern was the only real candidate in the race. We needed a big victory, 50%, said Frank, to give us a push toward California. But, as the only campaigning candidate in the race, shouldn't we expect to get more than half the Democratic votes? Apparently not. We got our 50%, followed by Wallace with 20%, and Humphrey with 13%; the same night, we also won in Rhode Island with 41% to Muskie's 21%, Humphrey's 20%, and Wal-

lace's 15%. The only problem, and it didn't bother anyone, was that in Rhode Island, only 10% of the state's
registered Democrats had voted. We had won 41% of
10%.

I was beginning to think we weren't winning the
nomination; we were getting it by default.

chapter 5

The $1,000
Misunderstanding

A campaign offers the attraction of instant recognition and fame. If you are in a key spot during a winning campaign, there is the possibility at any minute that your picture may be in the newspapers, *Time,* and *Newsweek.* You may be televised, quoted, and make important contacts never before possible. And then, there is the possibility of the White House job and more publicity and more contacts. Those attracted to these rewards are desperate to achieve them instantly because time is so short. It's their one chance to be noticed, and they must be noticed above all others. Ethics disappear. It isn't like a corporation where one's insidious efforts to dislodge the person in the next office may backfire, or, in time, be discovered. A campaign has no time. Whatever happens, you're suddenly on to a new state, new people. No one cares about injustices of the past, and the past is yesterday, no longer relevant. Within a campaign public opinion is influenced by power, not morals, which works to the advantage of the instigator, to the disadvantage of the victim. You can be destroyed, or you can get away with anything you try.

I thought of Rick Stearns, Assistant Campaign Director in charge of non-primary states, who had been quoted in a recent magazine article as saying, "Most political campaigns are built like the Austrian Empire —all the power is at the capital with anarchy thirty miles away. But we don't see enough of each other to start conspiracies." He must be crazy. There were conspiracies everywhere, rumors everywhere, and endless discussions of who would be fired.

I hadn't yet heard I would be fired, but there was a rumor around that I was certainly busy. Apparently, I had only gotten my job by sleeping with George McGovern. I was only keeping my job because of my consuming affair with Frank Mankiewicz and, if those two weren't enough, there was also, of course, my really torrid relationship with Pierre Salinger.

It was probably just my naïveté that caused these things to come as a surprise. Everyone hears about the viciousness of politics behind the scenes—even I had— but I'd always thought it was exaggerated, that if you were smart and didn't cause problems, those things would never happen to *you.*

But the stakes are too high in a political campaign for normal ethics to prevail.

I was puzzled by the first rumor. Why me? I wasn't even one of the staffers trying to look close to McGovern. Why wasn't it said about those who were constantly breathing down his neck or draping themselves over his shoulders? Simple. They were men. And Mankiewicz—Good God, I couldn't even get his *ear!* And Pierre—poor Pierre, the only man good-natured enough to give that speech in Port Huron, Michigan, or Lame Fang, Nevada, where no one else would go because it meant a plane at 5 a.m. with three stops and two connections at different airports. I no longer even *saw* him!

Where were Women's Lib and Gloria Steinem when

I needed them? Of course, there was nothing unique in all this. A woman has to go through it all the time, but particularly, apparently, in a political campaign. Ironically, to be chosen for the rumor in the first place is a compliment. It means you are doing a good enough or, at least, noticeable enough job to be a threat to someone, who then starts the rumor, to assure himself or herself and, hopefully, the world at large, that you couldn't possibly have been chosen for anything connected with your *head*. But there's also nothing you can do about it. To run about wildly proclaiming who it is you're *not* having an affair with merely confirms the suspicions of those who hadn't quite made up their minds and brings it to the attention of those who hadn't heard.

What was particularly absurd about this particular rumor was that the McGovern campaign was possibly the most sexless campaign in history. From what I had seen firsthand in three national campaigns for President (Robert Kennedy, Humphrey, and Nixon in 1968) and two in New York (Lindsay for Mayor and Carter Burden for Councilman), the normal campaign ambience seemed to be a fevered pitch of activity and excitement bordering on hysteria. In a national campaign, especially, you are caught in what can be for the candidate a life-and-death battle for top job in the world. Adrenaline pumps, energy pulsates, and nerves tense. Whether working for the candidate, writing about him, or merely observing, you are constantly keyed up by the pace, the feeling of power, and excitement over what might happen next. At the end of the day, where does all this pent-up energy go? To bed, of course, and not alone.

Like soldiers in a foxhole, unnatural relationships are

formed in a campaign. Bonds are quickly tied by virtue of shared experience and interest, and previous attachments fall away as your world diminishes. Home no longer exists; it has been replaced by something cozier and more engulfing—the campaign itself. Men who might seem most dreary when viewed with the full trappings of their lives—wife, children, and suburban home—are now only seen as much-needed and very available mental, emotional, and physical companions.

A phone call is made by the reporter to his wife (not every night) during which he whimpers about being on the "verge of total collapse from the constant strain and exhaustion of this wretched campaign." His wife hangs up with the impression that her poor husband has barely the strength to lift his head. She is wrong. On his end, the very action of replacing the receiver in its cradle infuses him with energy. He bounds into action. Guilt is gone.

In part, the campaign mood is set by the candidate. It doesn't matter if anything is actually going on, but whether it appears that it *could*. In the Kennedy campaign, for example, Bobby was seen in more than casual conversation with several beautiful young women, one of them a movie actress and conscientious worker who popped up again on the fringes of the McGovern campaign. And Steve Smith, Bobby's Campaign Manager, furthered the aura of mystery. He, himself, was an attractive figure, and there were attractive people around him. Anything was possible, and whether it was indeed happening or not made no difference. There was a sexy mood in the air. In fact, during Bobby's California primary, should fire have broken out in San Francisco's Fairmont Hotel, only ten people, at most, would have been found up in their own rooms.

86 ☐

While George McGovern seemed relatively single-minded for a politician, it was not impossible to distract him, but none of the intrigue was there. No one cared. And, of course, McGovern's concentration was aided by the presence of his lovely wife for much of the trip.

Gary Hart was more easily distracted from his nominal duties as Campaign Manager, forming close friendships with a movie star, a receptionist or two, and a bevy of female reporters constantly publicizing him. Because power is sexy, those close to it become surrogately sexy. And after all, those surrogates might as well enjoy it; since, after the election, should their candidate lose, they will undoubtedly discover that the musk they had been exuding while in the presence of Power, has evaporated forever.

The surrogate sex objects are desired mainly by other staffers, hoping for favors or the chance to get closer to Power themselves, and those women reporters who haven't been able to get their stories together in conventional interviews. By and large, however, the press and staff tend to stay in separate sexual camps for reasons of comfort and security.

For the male reporter, the available objects of choice are, of course, female reporters or staffers, and stewardesses. Stewardesses, however, tend to be risky for anyone except the short-term traveling reporter. There she is on the same plane day after day for a period of months, a bit of a drag should he tire of her affections. Female reporters, on the other hand, are usually along for short periods of time rather than the whole haul, and, if receptive and reasonably attractive, can have the choice of a planeload of men. He and she sit together, their schedules are the same, they share the same tenseness over having a story to file (when writing under pressure, it's also reassuring to have someone around to remind you of forgotten details), and when they have finally filed their stories, both feel an enormous sense of relief and release. They are finished for the day. They can now unwind together, have a few drinks, and eventually *sleep.*

And while they sleep, the poor staff workers are often huddled, red-eyed, in strategy meetings. Their phones can ring at any hour of the night (Frank Mankiewicz was very big on the 5:15 a.m. call); they may have to leap up and work on a schedule change, a speech, a press release, or any number of ghastly details which loom up at unpleasant hours. They are more uptight, nervous, and tired because, in effect, they can never file their stories. The story is on-going, 24 hours a day, perhaps for three-quarters of the year. On the McGovern campaign, particularly, they were also constantly worried about losing their jobs or being slandered by their fellow staff workers.

Besides being up half the night, the McGovern staffers were also boringly moralistic. In their eyes, our battle for the nomination was one of Good versus Evil. We were Right (From the Start) and we had God on our side. This conviction so filled them with a sense of Divine Mission that they found it almost impossible to form a relationship with anything short of another Divine Being. It made for a certain sexual prudishness.

But we were on our way to the "Superbowl of the primaries" as Humphrey called it—California, a very sexy state. Maybe all the rumors about me would come true.

The campaign was staying at the Wilshire Hyatt House, situated under a thick cloud of smog in the center of downtown Los Angeles, not your sexiest hotel, but at least one with air conditioning, a small pool on the roof, and an intoxicating mood of victory in the air. Frank was confident we'd win here, he said, because Californians are attracted to winners, not losers, and McGovern having just won two more primaries, was a winner.

McGovern had also been lucky. With the press on our side, we had driven through the primaries to California, but now in the Golden State that ride was to be stopped short by a wall of questions.

On Saturday, May 27, Ben Okner of the Brookings Institute, one of McGovern's economic advisors, held a press briefing to explain some of the specifics of McGovern's economic distribution program. If his intention was to tangle his remarks in such economic technologica that no one could understand them, he succeeded brilliantly. But the trouble was that, even though completely confused, the press had still managed to ask questions. And they hadn't gotten answers.

Neither had McGovern, for that matter. He had coasted to California without anyone knowing what his positions were, including himself. Now he was ready to abandon or, at least, drastically modify the ones on economics and defense, which were causing the most trouble. You can't, said Frank and Gordon. If you do that, they argued, you'll lose your credibility, and it's that credibility which has brought us all so close to victory. Better retain good credibility by sticking to bad positions.

Throughout the primaries thus far, the Mankiewicz-Weil approach had been for the Senator to stick to a policy of nonspecifics, which, in essence, boiled down to his saying, when pressed, "Anything is better than the current welfare mess." Now in California, several economic brains on hand to brief McGovern for his first televison debate against Humphrey the following afternoon strongly disagreed with that strategy. It had worked in New Hampshire, they said, where Mankiewicz could always divert attention from McGovern's blunders by a clever quip or two and where no one had been particularly interested in McGovern's economic or defense policies beyond how they immediately affected New Hampshire. "So far," one of them said, "McGovern's had been the least in-depth Presidential campaign imaginable." Now, in the three television debates, his programs would be held up to public scrutiny and they had better look good.

But at the CBS studio the next afternoon, nothing looked good. Humphrey's media advisor had to have been sick or he wouldn't have allowed Hubert to come to the studio wearing a mustard-colored shirt. Now a mustard shirt is just the very worst color you can wear on color television unless you're trying to win sympathy by looking like you have an upset stomach. McGovern, at least, was in the very best choice for color TV, light blue.

Humphrey didn't look good, nor was he in a good mood. Taking the offensive from the start, he began with the catchy McGovern phrase "Right from the Start," and suggested it be changed to "Wrong from the Start"—"wrong about Israel, wrong about unemployment compensation, wrong about the labor law, wrong about his unrealistic welfare program, about taxation, and wrong about national security."

To which McGovern replied that Humphrey wasn't

so right all the time either and quoted, to the accompaniment of much studio laughter, one of the Minnesotan's better-known past effusions, "Vietnam is a glorious adventure and what a wonderful one it is!"

McGovern looked calm and handsome and spoke well. His answers were slow and I thought, reasonable. Humphrey looked slightly hysterical and exceedingly yellow and shouted and waved his arms. McGovern was definitely doing better. And then it happened. "Senator McGovern has concocted a fantastic welfare scheme which will give everyone, even Nelson Rockefeller, $1,000, and it will cost the taxpayers 60 or 70 billion dollars," Humphrey sputtered. Panelist David Schumacher cleared his throat. "Exactly how much," he asked McGovern, "will your plan cost?" McGovern looked startled, as though, in the midst of a biology exam, he'd been asked to conjugate a French verb. His expression informed the viewer that neither the question nor its answer had ever passed through his mind.

"I honestly don't know," he said. "I don't have the figures."

"Oh, God," moaned two staffers in unison. "There it goes." They were not alone in their reaction. Later that night, a group of us came upon Gordon Weil outside the hotel press room. "George McGovern's gonna ruin me!" he was shouting rather drunkenly to anyone who would listen. "He's going to throw the campaign away after all I've done!" He turned to an imaginary figure in the hall—at least, I assumed it was imaginary because even with my glasses on I didn't see anyone there. "You're gonna have to start making up your mind," he yelled, shaking his finger violently at an invisible George McGovern, "I'm not gonna stand for this!"

Somewhere in the gloom of the hall, he must have glimpsed his future job as Secretary of the Treasury slipping away.

"I just wish the election was tomorrow instead of nine days from now," said Pat Caddell.

Working conditions in California were a definite improvement over the other states. Pat Caddell had enticed Barbara Runyon, the girl who had helped me in Ohio, and a friend of hers, Pat McFarland, to come to California to work for him, and now he loaned them to me. Our policy was to get up early, arrive at the office by 9:30, and work until 6:00. However, if it was a particularly sunny day, we would try to take a lunch break by the hotel pool from 2 to 3:30 and then return to work until 7 or so.

This plan ran counter to the artificial work ethic. In California, many top aides spent considerable time giving interviews to the press. The best spot for this, of course, was out by the pool or at one of the umbrella-ed tables on the veranda where they could discuss themselves over lunch and a few martinis. An interview fell into the category of work. But what if you weren't a man? No one ever interviewed a woman in the McGovern campaign; in fact, in this campaign, women only seemed to exist in bulk—committees of women set up to do thus and so. Therefore, since the three of us were never being interviewed, our forays into the sun were looked on as PLEASURE.

It is hard to enjoy an hour of anything, even sun, if you also have to cope with a constant round of passing remarks—"Well, I see you're taking it easy today . . ." "Sure wish my job afforded me such luxury . . ."

The most inconsistent thing of all was that those who

made the most remarks usually slept the latest, enjoyed a sumptuous breakfast in the dining room with an "important person" (work category), then retired to their rooms where they couldn't possibly be observed not working, and only came out for their luncheon interview. Most of the interviewees spent considerable time trying to convince the press how decentralized the campaign was. "No one," opined Gary Hart, "is really sure whether he's higher or lower than the man next to him." That might be true, but what Gary left out was that, not knowing, the bulk of them would then concentrate all their energies on becoming either indisputably higher or, at least, spreading the word that they were.

Even one of our big contributors, a San Franciscan named June Degnan, enthused in print, "This is the most competent campaign I've ever seen. George [McGovern] has a genius for organization. He has a marvelous sense of who can do what. And he lets them do it."

Then why was nobody doing it?

But what did it matter? The California Field Poll results were beyond our wildest dreams, showing us ahead of Humphrey by 20 points—46% to 26% with 10–12% undecided. "That's about right," Pat Caddell agreed. "That's what my poll came up with but I thought it was too good to be true."

The second debate was two days after the first, on NBC's "Meet the Press." This time, Humphrey had been placed in a blue shirt and looked considerably healthier. Platitudes dissolved, and a few facts took over. McGovern even came up with a figure for his income maintenance plan, albeit a bogus one. Right after the first debate, Ted Van Dyk, one of McGovern's chief issues advisors, had written a memo criticizing his handling of the money question and suggesting a short statement for him to make at the next debate, something to the effect that, "Having done further work, I've come up with an approximate cost of ———." He left a blank space for McGovern to fill in when he'd done the further work.

But in the car going over to NBC for the debate, Gordon Weil later told Van Dyk that researcher John Holum had quizzed McGovern about the new figures. McGovern didn't have any, but then as Gordon watched, the candidate pulled out Van Dyk's statement, gazed out of the car window for a moment, and quickly scribbled a number in the allotted space. Where did he get it? asked Van Dyk after the show. Out of the blue, said Gordon.

But after all, what could you expect? McGovern's economic innocence had a long history, showing itself for the first time in 1969 when he had rushed back to his Senate office after having lunch with a news correspondent, and said, "Sandy Vanocur says the economy is going to be a hot issue. We're going to have to do something about the economy." "What?" asked Weil. "Something," said McGovern.

And he came up with something, though pretty sketchily thought out. Casting about for some issues to add to McGovern's one-issue candidacy, Weil had thought up the now famous $1,000-a-person guaranteed income plan, which he was now stuck trying to defend. "What McGovern has proposed as figures are only suggestions," Gordon kept saying. "It's not anything we want to be locked into." The trouble was that no one in the campaign ever wanted to be locked into anything. Back in December 1971, several months before the New Hampshire primary, Mankiewicz had met with John Holum and Gordon Weil and asked them where they were planning to get the money to pay for the $1,000-a-person plan. Neither had a clue. Find out fast, said Mankiewicz. But then New Hampshire had come along, the campaign had gotten frantic, and it seemed easier to avoid the issue than cope with it, so the $1,000 income-maintenance proposal slipped into the economic package for good.

In McGovern's mind, there was no stigma attached to the answer, "I don't know." Actually, it was one of his favorite answers. It showed he was honest and gave him flexibility, a chance to keep options open and not be "locked in." And on this point, the staff agreed; they thrived on the confusion, a moving shield under which they could constantly maneuver and juggle without censure.

After months of confusion and occasional sabotage, I wondered if it were also possible this year to fix the polls? Something about the Field Poll, showing us ahead by 20 points, seemed bizarre. Bobby Kennedy had beaten Gene McCarthy by only 3 points in 1968, and that had been touted as a big victory by California standards. Could we have bought the poll? Or could someone else? Poor Muskie really had missed the boat, even from the very beginning, with his "Trust Muskie" posters. What a dumb idea to push—this wasn't the year to trust anyone.

Suspicions increased in California, but so did something else—the Kennedy influence. It was scarcely a concealed fact that McGovern craved a Kennedy endorsement, and more, wanted Kennedy to run as his Vice Presidential candidate. Now, with victory almost at hand, McGovern's thirst got stronger. Pat Caddell had been polling to determine which, if any, of a large selection of Vice Presidential possibilities had the right "image" to add votes to the ticket. Only Kennedy would be a definite plus, he found. But Kennedy wasn't cooperating. Not only was he not gobbling up the Vice Presidential offer, but he hadn't even gotten around to endorsing McGovern.

On June 3rd, three days before the primary, I traveled on the Senator's whistle-stop train ride through California. The McGoverns, their family and relatives, top staff, and chosen friends sat in the back car. Someone had sent a bottle of champagne and Eleanor McGovern held it on her knee. She looked very young and pretty in her blue and white checked pants suit with a big white corsage pinned to her blouse. Next to her sat her husband, jacket off, nibbling peanuts from a small cellophane package and staring out the window as the California countryside flashed by. Next to him, Shirley MacLaine, her face almost obscured by glasses and a large visored cap, scribbled frantically into her notebook. Around them, other staff members pushed back and forth, the top echelon trying to look as conspicuous as possible, the less-than-top trying to look as *in*conspicuous as possible so as not to be thrown out of the car by Gordon Weil, who had the habit, when the Senator was around, of always trying to clear a room.

I took pictures of McGovern being interviewed for a future *Life* magazine article and then sat down to talk to him myself. McGovern had a wonderful quality of accessibility. His staff could be clearing aisles and carting people bodily off but, if you wanted to talk to George McGovern, he would stop and listen. He had an easy smile and a serene just-about-to-be-amused expression which made him seem an island of normalcy in the midst of the rumor-ridden turmoil around him. I often stopped to talk to him just to calm my nerves. His closest staff called him "Senator," but I, although I didn't know him that well, always had to fight an impulse to call him "George."

"I hope you're going to drop that $1,000-for-every-one plan," I said. "I don't think it's working in the best interests of population control."

"Why is that?" he asked. "Because," I said, "if you offer a poor family a certain amount of money per person, that family might be tempted to keep adding persons."

McGovern looked surprised. "Kristi," he said very quietly, and he reminded me of my father, "people don't have children for reasons like that."

"But they do," I insisted, forgetting I was talking to a potential President, "I used to work in Harlem with unwed mothers and a lot of them had children just to get more welfare."

McGovern looked even more surprised, and I suddenly suspected that he had never worked in a ghetto. "That's interesting," he said. "I'm not sure you're right, but I'll think about it." I believed he would.

Before today's train ride, McGovern had spoken movingly about visiting Cesar Chavez, head of the United Farmworkers Union, who had endorsed him, and whose cause Bobby Kennedy had supported in 1968. He intended to reiterate his own support of Chavez during the whistle-stop tour. But two stops before Delano, Chavez' United Farmworkers headquarters, a delegation of California growers got on the train. Chavez isn't just up against the big guys, they said, he's also hurting the small farmers like us. You'll lose us if you support him. The Delano stop came and went and McGovern never mentioned Chavez. "It's an example of how easy it is to manipulate him," muttered one unhappy aide. "He's swayed by the last person he talks to."

The next few days were filled with rallies, fund raisers, radio and television tapings, and the last debate the Sunday before the primary—this time on ABC–TV with an expanded cast of characters, including Los Angeles Mayor Sam Yorty and New York Congresswoman Shirley Chisholm, shown by split screen from the East.

Shirley Chisholm, reminding everyone she was "the dark horse of the race, literally and figuratively," lent an air of levity and common sense somewhat missing from the previous debates, while Sam Yorty, whose nationwide ratings had dropped from 2% to 1% in recent weeks, was unable to get a single sentence together without some mistake.

"I'm the Mayor of by far the largest city in Los Angeles," he said, emphatically assessing his qualifications for the Presidency.

Humphrey and McGovern argued over which of them had shown greater support for Israel and the SST.

"I'm the only one here wearing a POW bracelet," said Yorty. Humphrey and McGovern hammered away on Social Security and defense spending.

"I've been Mayor of the largest state for eleven days," insisted Yorty, losing patience.

It all comes down to the question, said Humphrey, "of whether the American people want a welfare program that puts no emphasis on work?" Even after the debate was over, Humphrey's question continued to hang in the California air.

That night, I went to a fund-raising party in Benedict

Canyon given by actress Marlo Thomas. The guests (anyone who had received an invitation and sent in money) stood somewhat motionlessly in clusters around the terraced pool and the sprawling green lawn, where a number of women—who appeared to have rented outfits from the same agency—stood eyeing each other in their full-length chiffon dresses, ribboned bonnets, and parasols. They held Chihuahuas instead of purses and looked utterly ill at ease. Warren Beatty, in steel-rimmed glasses, turtleneck, and jacket, stood with the hostess, Marlo Thomas, nervously brushing his shoulder-length brown hair from his eyes, looking like Gary Hart (who had come to look just like Warren Beatty), while a long line of people waited wordlessly by the buffet table and photographers wandered from group to group, not wanting to waste film but being quite sure who deserved a picture.

The whole thing had an unreal quality to it; but then, nothing seemed just right anymore. It was a closely guarded secret that our 20-point margin in the polls was slipping, and for the first time, McGovern's supremely confident staff felt the stirrings of fear. They were beginning to get edgy. "I just wish it were over," Pat Caddell kept saying.

Through the primaries, McGovern and his staff had been running like a group of lemmings with blinders on, toward the sea, which, in their case, happened to be The Nomination. The Nomination was their only goal, a goal now out of all proportion because McGovern's long-shot candidacy had made it seem unattainable. And because it had seemed unattainable, McGovern now credited it with mystical powers. If he won The Nomination, he would somehow become invincible and have anything he wanted.

His staff, however, did not see him as potentially invincible. Instead, as McGovern got closer to the cherished nomination, it was clear that the candidate had simply become a puppet for his staff's ambitions. As long as he could repeat Mankiewicz' jokes, continue the Kennedy myth, and keep up his "Honest George" appearance, that was fine with them, but they didn't want him to muddle up the campaign. They really wanted a Kennedy-faced Charlie McCarthy, not a real live Presidential candidate called George McGovern. Because if anything went wrong, those White House jobs, which all of them seemed to believe they already had, could go right down the drain.

And there was another fear, too. Should McGovern falter now under their tutelage, it opened the dread possibility that he might then seek wiser counsel. And that counsel was waiting, and not breathing too softly, in the wings. It took several forms—the shapeless ones of former Muskie, Lindsay, and McCarthy advisors who had been lurking about the campaign fringes waiting for a weak link or an expanded chain to let them in, and the specific forms of Dick Dougherty, talented but as yet untitled "press liaison," and Fred Dutton, former top Kennedy aide turned McGovern advisor who had been McGovern's first choice for campaign director before Mankiewicz. It seemed logical now that Dutton and Dougherty might take over from their less experienced counterparts. Press liaison Dougherty might be asked to ease Kirby Jones from his Press Secretary slot and Dutton, who had held the same job with Robert Kennedy as Gordon Weil had with McGovern, could do the same. One oft-repeated staff joke, in fact, measured the amount of time it took Weil to reach McGovern's side when he saw him talking to Dutton: It ranged from

100 □

7 to 10 seconds. "We can't let the heavies destroy our thing," they all said. It was one matter on which the McGovern staff agreed.

But the upheaval had begun. The heavies were joining the bandwagon; Senators Frank Church (Idaho), Abraham Ribicoff (Connecticut), and John Tunney (California) had jumped on in California, and rumors were back that Hart would soon be fired. He had clashed with Dutton, they said, and in California, Dutton was the heavy, his opinions being give more and more credence by the now diminishing Field Poll. Gary, said Fred, ". . . was trying to run a grassroots campaign in a media state. But instead of an amateur army, he now had masses of pushy young men knocking on doors, trying to show the strength of the McGovern machine. McGovern doesn't understand," he said, "that the nomination doesn't mean a damn thing if you antagonize everyone getting it and that there's no point getting off the ground if you're going to crash land." Dutton was also against spending the last days of the campaign in the northern part of the state, already our stronghold, and wasting yet another day on a Kennedy copy, the whistle-stop train ride. "No one seems to realize," he kept saying, "that Humphrey's taken over our underdog role. California's turning around and we're going down."

But Gary Hart had weathered these storms before. In the words of one top advisor in from the start, "Gary was always a yes man in a political holding position." Back in December 1971, McGovern had announced that Mankiewicz would be Campaign Manager and chief spokesman, Gary would go out in the field, and Ted Van Dyk, a Humphrey aide in 1964 and 1968, would do issues and research. But Gary wouldn't go out in the field; instead, said the aide, "He sat there worrying about his positions and signing letters, 'Gary Hart, Campaign Manager.' " Then at the time of the Wisconsin primary, McGovern had again announced the same decision; Frank would be Campaign Manager and Gary would go out in the field—news which Joe Grandmaison had disseminated during the Wisconsin victory celebration. But again, Gary had simply stayed on and kept signing letters. Apparently, Mankiewicz had never made an issue of it. Instead, he pulled a new title out of the hat for himself—"National Political Director" —and things went on as usual.

The day before the election, McGovern's schedule was suddenly scrapped in midmorning, and he took off for Texas to try to head off a stop-McGovern movement by a group of Southern governors. "It's just the very worst thing he could do," said Shirley MacLaine. "When that hits the news, it'll look like we were so sure of victory we couldn't be bothered with California the last day of the race. It looks like we're taking the state for granted, and I know Californians—they won't like it one bit."

Election Night was run with maximum security, and it took three assorted badges just to get upstairs to our Situation Room in the manager's office on the third floor. I walked in to find Pierre, with Miles Rubin and Eli Segal, the California coordinators, staring gloomily at the television screen from which had just come the announcement that judging from the first returns, the election was too close to call. It looked as though Fred Dutton and Shirley MacLaine might be right.

Some Southern precincts started coming in: a blue-collar district in Orange County's Garden Grove with 82 for Humphrey, 43 for McGovern; Anaheim with 75 for Humphrey, 37 for McGovern. Frank arrived, unsmiling. There was little conversation, great tenseness, and disbelief. Had our 20% slipped away to nothing?

Finally came the first statewide percentages and the room brightened: 41.3% for McGovern, 40.8 for Humphrey; and a short time later, NBC projected McGovern the winner.

Frank and Pierre squeezed Miles Rubin, stood up, and looking rather misty-eyed, put their arms around each other.

"We are deeply grateful to everyone who has worked with us for this wonderful night," said McGovern. "And I am confident that the same fresh spirit, the same devoted effort, the same sense of a greater vision of this country will carry us to victory at Miami and again this November, and then most important of all, in the White House on behalf of all Americans." And then he quoted Robert Kennedy: "What we need most of all in this country is for each of us to believe again that one man or one woman can make a difference. We can change the direction of this country if only you and I have the courage to stay involved."

I had believed it once. Why couldn't I believe it again? I wondered whether McGovern did. It was all beginning to sound like rhetoric. His words were meaningful but they seemed to apply to some other campaign in some other time. I felt no stirring in my gut, nothing except a vague discontent and sadness.

Pierre, Frank, and I walked out to the car where Pierre took me aside. "The Senator has promised that if we get the nomination I'll be Chairman of the DNC," he said, "and if I do, I want you to work with me."

It didn't sound bad or good, just a long way off.

Back at the hotel, I went to work in our second Situation Room where, at 1:30 a.m., NBC gave our final victory percentage—45% to 40% (which would later be adjusted to 44.3% to 39.2%), a five-point spread, 15% less than the polls had indicated.

Pierre stuck his head in the door. "They're going to say that when people realized what McGovern's policies really were, they decided to vote for Hubert Humphrey," he said. "You'd better point out that this is the biggest spread in voting there has ever been in a California Presidential primary."

We had only one uncontested primary, in New York, to go. Despite some temporary setbacks, the battle plan had worked.

chapter 6

High Tide
at Miami Beach

I was happy to get back to New York, to see my friends from the outside world, and to finally spend the night in my own bed. Ahead of me stretched twelve blissful days of working in the New York headquarters, which I thought had to be less strife-ridden than the Washington office.

And it was. I had two jobs—putting together Election Night procedures and helping to organize Warren Beatty's big Madison Square Garden McGovern rally the following week. This time, I wouldn't have to do a key precinct analysis because it was a different kind of primary; slates of delegates to the Convention would be elected by district on Primary Day—248 of them—with an additional 28 Delegates-at-Large to be chosen 3 days later by the Democratic State Committee.

Again, McGovern was almost unopposed. Humphrey had never filed slates of delegates and Muskie, Jackson, and Chisholm had so few as not to count. McGovern's only slight opposition came from several slates of "Uncommitteds." Now the only question was how many delegates of the possible 248 he would get. As it had done to Muskie in New Hampshire, the Press in New York made daily predictions and arrived at arbitrary figures.

☐ *107*

The Madison Square Garden rally the week before the primary was a sellout and the crush was on for free press tickets. For the first time, I found myself in the position of having information and favors to dispense rather than to grapple for, and it was a heady experience. I found it easy to turn people down and to maintain a granitelike resolve, even though the lady reporter from *Sewing Circle Magazine* on the other end of the phone insisted, absolutely insisted, that she truly intended to run a major political piece the following month and *Women's Wear Daily* warned me that the ruin of their article would fall on my head if I allowed them only one reporter instead of two.

The night of the rally I had the best job of all—checking press credentials, letting the Right people in and keeping the Wrong people out. It was terrible to admit, of course, but I loved every minute of it. There they were, girl friends of accredited reporters trying to sneak in as "assistants" and photographers; little old ladies in oxford shoes wearing raveled "TV Crew" credentials, obviously found in the street; twitchy office workers claiming to represent major newspapers whose editors had apparently forgotten to inform me of their planned arrival; fat men with calling cards imprinted *Gardening Today Magazine* not to mention a sizable group of legitimate guests and reporters whose names just didn't happen to appear on the list. *I* held all their fates in my hands, and *I* could reject them.

Along came a reporter for *The Daily News*. Her name wasn't on the list. In the old days, I would have checked her press card and let her in. But now, after 5 months with the McGovern staff, I had changed.

"Your name's not on the list," I sneered. She became angry—then furious. I sighed the McGovern staff sigh.

"Please step aside," I said in a bored tone, "I'll attend to the problem after all these other people come in."

Up came Blair Sabol of *The Village Voice* and Tim Crouse from *Rolling Stone*. Neither were on the list but they should have been—I liked them. I let them in.

The theme of the rally was "Coming Together," a bit too sophisticated a concept, perhaps, for the minister's son from South Dakota who became rather tangled in semantics during his opening remarks. But overall, the evening was a huge success; we raised half a million dollars, and the mood of victory was even thicker in the air.

Afterward, there was a big private dinner party at the Four Seasons Restaurant. Pierre Salinger, who was celebrating his birthday, took me along with his 21-year-old daughter, Suzanne, and son, Marc. Again, sweeping into the restaurant while flashbulbs popped and onlookers gaped, I felt a surge of pleasure at being In instead of Out.

Later that week, I had dinner with Pierre, who seemed distracted. He had seen Jean Westwood in Utah just after the California primary and she had casually told him that McGovern had promised her the job of Chairman of the DNC that he had earlier promised Pierre. Pierre had mumbled an "isn't that nice" response and shortly afterward had talked to McGovern in Washington. Once again McGovern had reaffirmed his promise to Pierre, telling him not to worry about Westwood. But Pierre seemed bothered nonetheless.

Three days before the Election, an interesting thing happened. A group of five men with guns and electronic surveillance equipment, wearing rubber gloves, had been caught inside the Democratic National Committee headquarters at the Watergate building in

Washington. Some were Cubans, but one of them, James McCord, had connections with the White House and the CIA. A friend called me the minute he heard the news on the radio. "This is it," he said excitedly, "it's the big break McGovern needs. When everything that must be behind that break-in gets out, you've got the election sewed up!" And had Watergate happened six months earlier, he might have been right.

Election Night was a haze of figures, none of which were clear until the final returns came in, but by the end of the night, we had won 230 of the 248 delegates, a definite victory by all standards. As in the Rhode Island primary, however, we had won in New York with the vote of only about 10% of the state's registered Democrats. Of that 10% vote, McGovern's delegates had gotten about two-thirds. In other words, we were off to Miami with the support of about six and one-half percent of New York State's registered Democratic voters. The primaries were over; we had gobbled up the uncontested ones; but it was not a matter of interest to anyone that we had never won a contested primary by as great a margin as Muskie's nine-point "defeat" in New Hampshire.

Back in Washington two days later, we got some good news. Muskie's former Campaign Manager, Berl Bernhard, had called Frank to say that Muskie had decided to announce his endorsement of McGovern at a speech the following day, Friday, June 9, at the National Press Club in Washington. In return, we would help absorb some of his campaign debts. Later in the afternoon, Bernhard called back. Muskie was getting some pressure not to endorse McGovern so he'd have to ponder some more and make a more "final" decision overnight. As it turned out, Muskie awoke with the final "final" decision, which was not to endorse McGovern after all.

Everyone was disappointed, but we could get along without Muskie. By our calculations, we now had 1,350 delegates, only 159 away from the magic 1,509 to win The Nomination. We had it almost locked up.

Almost. Now began a week of daily announcements of our ever-increasing number of pledged delegates. Finally, on June 26, the big moment came with McGovern's claim that "delegate pledges from black leaders leave no question that I'm over the top." This triumphant moment was somewhat diminished later that afternoon, however, by Rick Stearns' admission that District of Columbia Congressman Walter Fauntroy's pledge to deliver 160 black delegates had been just a bit hasty and that we were still just where we had been, almost over the top. It was the second disappointment.

Then three days later, we gathered around the television set at headquarters to watch the voting of the Democratic Credentials Committee on the California challenge. That winner-take-all primary, the Humphrey forces said, had been illegal according to McGovern's own reform rules which insisted on proportional representation to the Convention. That meant, in their opinion, that McGovern should receive delegates only in proportion to his 44.3% of the vote, Humphrey according to his 39.2%, and the also-rans in proportion to theirs. If Humphrey won the challenge, McGovern would lose 151 of his 271 California delegates.

At first, no one had taken the California challenge seriously. We had always won our battles despite heavy odds and the headquarters staff assumed we would do it again. There was stunned silence following the Credentials Committee vote of 72 to 66 in favor of stripping McGovern of his 151 California delegates.

"It'll be reversed by the Supreme Court," everyone agreed, and, "certainly on the floor of the Convention," but, nonetheless, it was a third disappointment, a genuine momentum-stopper, and it was momentum that had kept us going. The vote also revealed the depth of distaste many strong Democratic leaders felt toward McGovern, and the bitterness, now replaced by glee, of state leaders who, during caucuses in their own states, had been pushed aside by bused-in McGovern supporters.

"Today's events endanger McGovern's chances of nomination very little," said Mankiewicz solemnly. "What is endangered is his election. This was not a very edifying spectacle to put before the American people."

Most of the staff left the handling of the credentials problem in the capable hands of Mankiewicz, Hart, and Stearns while they went back to the more important work of back-biting.

The major news of the next few days concerned reactions and tactics on the California challenge. But another piece of news which eased itself out across the AP wire caught my attention. According to an "informed source," McGovern was planning to appoint a new Chairman of the Democratic National Committee— Jean Westwood. We were about to witness the decline and fall of the National Political Coordinator, Pierre Salinger. Another job title would soon be free.

I had been gone from the Washington office for a month, and during my absence there had been some changes. A new girl, Sarah, a tall brunette in her thirties, had joined our overfilled office and was now in charge of "Convention arrangements." She was working closely with Angel and their inseparableness was comparable to that of Betsey and Bobbie, who had now almost merged into a single shape.

Since I had never attended a Convention, I was rather curious to know what it might be like, but details were not forthcoming. Phone calls to Miami were made in hushed tones, lists were immediately concealed in file folders, and the entire coming event was shrouded in mystery. Sarah kept all her information in a big, black, spiral notebook, which I was amazed to find her carting to the ladies' room, to the refrigerator, and even to a restaurant for lunch. My curiosity about its contents began to consume me. "What's in the notebook?" I asked, yawning in a disinterested sort of way. "Things," she said.

In his cubicle, Steve Robbins was wreathed in smiles. He had a secret. Actually, he had two secrets—when the staff plane would leave for Miami and when the Senator's plane would leave. He had a third secret, too —who would get to go on which plane. Sarah and Angel also had a secret—who would be privileged to stay at which hotel. I, as usual, had no secrets—and fewer answers.

There was some secret typing going on, too—a biography of "certain" staff members which would be included in Convention kits given to delegates and press. Everyone, naturally, wanted to be on the list, but no one could find out whether he was, who else was, who was compiling the list, or where it could be found. It magnified the already rampant unrest.

And the biggest secret of all still remained—what was Henry Kimelman doing with our money? I had been getting my regular salary every two weeks but had now expended some $600 of my own money in expenses and plane tickets traveling around the country for two months of almost weekly primaries.

"We just don't have the money," Marian Pearlman said, arranging her face in a combination sad-sincere expression, "but, of course, we'll pay you back when we do."

Just before the Fourth of July, there was a major unveiling—a portion of the black notebook—when for the first time I saw a neatly typed sheet with all our names and after them an initial designating the hotels where we would stay. After Sarah, there was a "D" (for Doral, luxury hotel for McGovern and staff), after Angel, a "D," after Margie, a "D," after Bobbie and Betsey and Steve Robbins, "D's." After Witker, there was a "Clar."

"What's the Clar?" I asked nervously, feeling that knot in my stomach which always came on when Angel smiled or began to purr, and she was suddenly smiling and purring at once.

"Oh," she said, "that's a really nice hotel on the beach called the Claridge." Well, it sounded sort of English and maybe it wouldn't be bad; besides, the elevator service would certainly be better than at the Doral since the Claridge was bound to be less crowded.

There was one piece of good news, in my mind anyway, which was that Gary Hart had persuaded Frank that our headquarters was too small for a national campaign. After the Convention, we would move to larger, more centrally located space—Muskie's old headquarters at 1910 K Street, which during his campaign had been renumbered as 1972 K Street.

114 ☐

We were to fly to Miami on a staff plane on Thursday, July 6. Two days before, on the afternoon of July 4, I took the shuttle to New York to pick up some clothes for Miami, returning to Washington early the next morning.

"The staff plane's been canceled," Teresa, the receptionist, announced cheerfully when I walked in. "Everyone left by bus at eight this morning."

Obviously, I had missed the bus. But a 28-hour bus ride would not exactly land one in Miami in the best shape to start a round-the-clock job, anyway. I would take another plane.

"Sorry," said Marion Pearlman, "the bus was free but if you fly, you'll have to pay for it yourself." "But I don't have any money," I said, "and no one told me they were canceling the plane."

"That's what happens when you take a half day off," she smirked.

On Thursday morning, I paid my fare with my American Express card, hoped for a computer error that would result in its being billed to someone else, and settled down on Eastern's flight to Miami. Next to me was Harold Himmelman, giving an interview. "Yes," he was saying, "we canceled the staff charter flight, but we suddenly got a big influx of money so no one had to pay his own way or go down to Miami on the bus."

Everything in Miami was 100 that day—the humidity and the temperature. Limply, I fell into a taxi. "To the Claridge," I said.

"The what?"

"The Claridge, you know, on Collins Avenue." The driver looked stupefied. It occurred to me that the Cla-

☐ *115*

ridge was possibly not your biggest, most centrally located hotel. And I was right. It was only after asking four people on the taxi's two-way radio that the driver was able to find it. And it was almost called the "Clar," but due to an electrical failure in the sign, it had instead become the "Ridge."

It was a small, rundown building on the side of the street where the beach was not, and it had no pool. It also had no room telephones, no maid service, no dining facilities, and almost no air conditioning. Under other circumstances, you might have said the hotel was closed for the summer. I pulled my suitcase out of the cab and stumbled up the steps to a small desk with no one at it. But there were sounds of life upstairs, a great deal of hammering and pounding. I moved in that direction and came upon a workman trying to extract his arm from an enormous hole in the wall.

"We're doing a lot of repairs," he said, eyeing my suitcase, "I didn't know anyone was staying here."

Eventually, I found my room on the second floor. It had two beds in it, one of which was unmade—vacated in a hurry, I later found out, by a less-than-satisfied guest—and a small window on whose glass pane the sun was beating to create an interesting sauna effect. There was no way I could survive eight nights.

Since I couldn't call our press suite at the Doral (no phone), I engaged the services of a public transport bus which, in due course, deposited me at the elegant, ornate-lobby'd Doral, where on the mezzanine floor, overlooking the pool, palm trees, and the sparkling blue sea (and air conditioned to an artic extent) was the press suite. And at comfortable desks around the room sat Dick Dougherty, Pierre Salinger, Margie, an elderly stern-faced woman I'd never seen before, and Sarah.

116 ☐

Dick Dougherty was sympathetic. "There's been some mistake," he said, "you can't stay in a place like that." But the assignments had been made, and now there was only one person who could change them, a man rewarded for his unfailing competence in past primaries, Larry Hotel.

Finally on top again after several misfortunes, Larry Hotel was not about to part with his power too hastily. "There are absolutely no rooms at the Doral," he said, "except those fifteen which are being saved for fat cats." There was a long pause. "But since Dougherty wants you to have one, *maybe* in a few days when Kathleen Kennedy gets here, you can share one with her."

"I will have roasted to death in a few days," I said.

"Yeah, maybe in a few days," he replied.

I did not sleep that night. The next morning, at 7, I waited at the bus stop, engulfed by humidity and mounting desperation, eager to luxuriate in a few air-conditioned moments at the Doral. And that day I got my assignment. I was not going to work at the Doral but at the Fontainebleau, the Convention headquarters hotel, a few blocks down Collins Avenue. I would manage the press operation there along with some press agent from New York. That sounded all right, and for a moment, I thought happily that perhaps I could now spend nights at my desk. So off I went to the Fontainebleau where networks, newspapers, magazines, and virtually every organization imaginable were busily setting up booths and elaborate work areas enclosed by blue muslin curtains. But there was no place for me.

None of the people in charge at the Fontainebleau, it turned out, had ever heard of a McGovern press operation to be set up in their midst. They needed a permit for every booth or cubicle and they hadn't gotten one from the McGovern campaign. Nor did they have any tables, telephones, or unused space sitting around for such a purpose. I returned to the Doral with the news. The New York press agent, however, having told everyone he knew about his interesting job with the McGovern press operation at the Fontainebleau was determined there should be one. He swept into action. And usually, if you want something badly enough you can get it, or at least part of it.

What he got was permission to put a small table with wobbly legs, in the hotel's only remaining available space—at the end of a dark hall in the basement, beyond the *Baltimore Sun's* curtain-enclosed cubicle. There was no telephone and little light. My job was to sit at the desk all day and hand out a pile of mimeographed day-old McGovern position papers. "I'll pick you up at five," the press agent said, and he was gone.

Here I was at my first exciting political convention—in a basement. I was tired from not sleeping the night before, I was starting to get a sore throat, and I felt very, very sorry for myself. I wanted my mother. But I couldn't get my mother without a telephone. The *Baltimore Sun* had telephones, however, and a very nice typewriter repairman who said I could use one. I dialed Connecticut.

"Hello," said Mother. "It's raining here, but I suppose you're having wonderful weather in Florida."

"I don't know," I said. "It's very hot, and I'm in a basement." And then it all came flooding out. "I'm absolutely miserable," I wailed.

"Well, dear," she said, not grasping the extent of my agony, "I tried to warn you in April . . . but you just wouldn't listen . . ."

118 □

fore riding in a South Dakota parade, George McGovern spruces up
Western look with a suede jacket from a local Custer store.

Bowling was the big
in the Wisconsin pri
and skilled or not,
candidate took an o
tunity to make a fool of
self for the photograp
It's Hubert Humph
turn here.

En route to a Milwa
factory during the Wi
sin primary, Major
Lindsay talked to the
thor. "There really
switch on to Lindsay,
said.

Kristi Witker

Owen Fra

Kristi Witker

Kristi Witker

Gordon Weil, McGovern's traveling advisor, shown in happier days. By the end of the convention, Fred Dutton had his job.

Frank Mankiewicz gets off the telephone for a moment to acknowledge his 48th birthday at the Washington campaign headquarters. The cake was baked by his assistant, Pat Broun, but another staffer took the credit.

Kristi Witker

Kristi Witker

Campaign manager, Gary Hart (at top) was a short-haired Denver boy when he began working for McGovern. By the end of the campaign he began to look suspiciously like Warren Beatty (below).

Owen Franken

While the bands play downstairs, members of the McGovern staff begin their weekly election night routine gathering returns in the primary states. Above, Massachusetts on April 4, 1972. From left to right: Kirby Jones, Pat Caddell, Kristi Witker, Gary Hart, Dan Porter, Frank Mankiewicz.

Kristi Witker

Eleanor McGovern laughs with Fred Dutton on a whistle-stop train ride before the California primary. One of McGovern's closest advisors, Dutton finally fell from favor after writing too many depressing memos.

Kristi Witker

Press Secretary Dick Dougherty watches his future White House job slip away as he listens to Tom Eagleton reveal his medical history at a press conference near Custer, South Dakota, July 25, 1972.

The last campaign stop of the day over, *Los Angeles Times* correspondent Jules Witcover relaxes on the *Dakota Queen* with the stewardesses. Witcover is now with the *Washington Post*.

Kristi Witker

Kristi Witker

While the candidate prepares for an important New Jersey rally with Ted Kennedy, the press covers the story from the motel. Left to right: Doug Kneeland of *The New York Times,* Jane O'Reilly from *New York* magazine, and Paul Hope of The *Washington Star.*

Owen Franken

The author on the campaign trail with Senator McGovern.

The Zoo plane, decorated with a Halloween motif, was home for much of the press corps.

Kristi Witker

The candidate in an airborne chat with actress Shirley MacLaine.

Kristi Witker

Football takes precedence over campaign pranks as Dick Tuck (right) settles down on a motel bed to watch TV with *Los Angeles Times* correspondent John Goldman.

Just before Tom Eagleton came along to put a damper on his Black Hills vacation, McGovern enjoyed an evening of song at the Sylvan Lake Lodge with researcher John Holum and personal secretary, Pat Donovan.

NBC correspondent Jack Perkins clowns in author's blonde wig.

Kirby Jones sits dejectedly in McGovern trailer outside Convention Hall. He had just lost his job as Press Secretary.

As a convention floor leader, Pierre Salinger worked long and slept little. A few days later he lost his promised job as Co-Chairman of the Democratic National Committee.

Frank Mankiewicz announced to a hushed press conference in Miami Beach McGovern's choice of Senator Thomas Eagleton as his running mate.

Eagleton's press conference in South Dakota has just ended. So, in effect, has George McGovern's campaign.

Kristi Witker

The candidate relaxing with friends and aides near the lodge where he was vacationing in the Black Hills of South Dakota.

Kristi Witke

The closest George McGovern came to having Ted Kennedy on the ticket was sharing the stage with him at an occasional rally. And the closest he came to the White House was the cake at right presented to him on his 50th birthday during his Black Hills "vacation."

Halloween at New York's Biltmore Hotel was a happy night as the staff, press, and secret service banded together to give the McGoverns a party on their 29th wedding anniversary.

Kristi Witker

Seven days later the campaign was over. McGovern delivers his concession speech at Sioux Falls Coliseum, November 7, 1972.

Kristi Witk

The conversation did not help a whole lot. I hung up and groped my way back to the desk. Frank had been right—this really was a once-in-a-lifetime experience, but it was one I now didn't think I could get through. I started to cry. And cry. I could have slashed my wrists, for that matter—certainly I wouldn't have bothered anybody, since no one, absolutely no one was passing through the Fountainbleau basement that day.

The next morning, I went back to the Doral press room to change assignments. I had not slept again and my throat was worse. Neither Pierre or Dick were in evidence, only the grim-faced older woman who, to my knowledge, had not been involved in the campaign before but who, I was told, had been "very big with the Kennedys."

"I'm in charge here," she said, "and you're supposed to be over at the Fontainebleau." Assuming she couldn't know, I told her about the desk in the basement and the stupidity of putting someone at it who could be doing some real work somewhere else.

"Well, this is my operation," she said, looking very menopausal. "Everyone else is being cooperative about their jobs. I don't see why you have to complain about yours."

It was futile. Frank and Gary were off fighting the California challenge, Pierre and Dick were involved in meetings outside the hotel, and as usual, no one of any ability was left in charge. But I didn't feel well enough to fight. I crept back to the basement.

On Monday evening, the first night of the Convention, Miss Menopause passed out credentials for the very important job of working in one of the three McGovern trailers outside Convention Hall. During the 4 nights the Convention would be in session, the trailers would be the nerve center of the McGovern operation, equipped with Telex and copying machines outside and inside telephones for constant contact with the floor leaders, and virtually everything else the operation might need.

Besides two operations-tactics trailers, there was also one for press so that additional copies of speeches, releases, delegate counts—whatever—could be run off and quickly distributed, and four privileged people from our office would spend the first night there. Needless to say, I was not one of them. Those who had gotten the nod from Miss Menopause strutted about the Doral press room wearing clumsy cardboard tags that said "Service," which I thought made them look awfully menial but they didn't seem to notice. Off they went to their first big night of the Convention, the biggest night of all, actually, because tonight would be the vote on the California challenge. If we won that, and we expected to, we would have enough votes for a first ballot nomination. The actual nomination two nights later would really be only a formality.

Before he had vanished from sight, Pierre had explained our tactics for the voting on the first challenge to come up Monday night, South Carolina, whose delegation had been challenged on the grounds that it did not include enough women. McGovern, that morning, had promised the women's caucus his "full and unequivocal support" of the challenge. But, said Pierre, the most important thing was to avoid the possibility of a floor test over what constituted a majority. On the California challenge, Chairman Larry O'Brien had ruled in our favor that 1,433, the majority of those eligible to vote, rather than 1,509, the absolute majority of the Convention, would constitute the majority vote on that challenge.

For the South Carolina challenge, the majority of those eligible to vote would be 1,496. The important thing, therefore, was to either win by more than 1,509 or lose by under 1,496, to avoid at all costs letting the vote fall into the "twilight zone" between 1,496 and 1,509. Because, if that happened, there would be a floor test on what constituted a majority and, should the test come up at the time of the South Carolina challenge, the entire California delegation (including its 151 anti-McGovern delegates) could vote in favor of making the majority 1,509, which would be to our disadvantage when the California vote came up later.

Those of us left behind in the press room, along with *Time* magazine's Don Wilson and Hugh Sidey, sat down to watch the tactic unfold. And it went off as scheduled. As the vote on South Carolina reached perilously close to the 1,496 boundary, a funny thing started happening. Delegation spokesmen started raising their hands and changing their votes. The women's challenge was defeated; the floor test didn't come up; and we had greatly strengthened our position for the vital California vote. Interviewed on the floor right after the vote, Pierre looked blank. He didn't have a clue as to what had happened, he said. Frank denied we had in any way manipulated the vote, and Gary Hart, with a quizzical-sincere look on his face, expressed genuine hurt that anyone could even think such a ghastly thing.

And they fooled almost everyone, including most of the network wizards who kept referring to the tremendous setback for the McGovern forces. The truth was that, while pretending to support the women on the

□ *121*

challenge in order to ensure the women's much-needed support on the California vote, the McGovern forces had adroitly pulled the rug out from under them. "Sure, we were willing to sell the women out," said Rick Stearns later, "but the whole thing was so complicated they never caught on."

We won the California challenge, and the staff members in the press room jumped up and down cheering. But I felt strangely let down. I had thought I'd be relieved since this was, after all, the moment we had ostensibly been working for. But instead, I was once again depressed.

"I hope you'll never tell anyone this," whispered Mike, a volunteer who had been drinking quietly through the vote, "but I'm miserable. I've been pushed around so much during this campaign that I was secretly hoping we'd lose the challenge so maybe the whole thing would just stop. Winning the nomination means all this viciousness will go on another four months."

The next day, I made a resolution. I, too, was tired of being pushed around. If I was going to sleep in a rathole at night, no way would I spend the day in a basement. So I moved back to the Doral press room, ignored Miss Menopause, and busied myself giving out issues and schedule information. It gave me a chance to see exactly what had been going on in my absence. What had been going on was very little. About three people worked hard; one was Margie, one was a serious political science major who had recently joined the campaign, and one was Miss Menopause. Everyone else tried to look busy while keeping a furtive eye out for the approach of television cameras.

The Doral press suite was one of the most accessible areas of the campaign. The more sensitive political operations under the direction of Mankiewicz, Hart, and Stearns were up on the hotel's 16th and 17th floors where McGovern had his suite and where the omnipresent Secret Service guarded all entrances. But almost anyone could come into the press room and usually did. That included newspaper and magazine reporters and endless TV crews, anxious to get a few interesting feet of film of McGovern staffers at work. And naturally, everyone wanted to be in those few feet, which made for a certain reluctance to leave the room, lest one's absence coincide with a film crew's arrival.

That morning as I sat talking on the telephone rather unbusily, I watched an ABC crew come in with a television camera trained on Margie's desk. Suddenly, Angel appeared at the door. Casually, ever so casually, she walked over to Margie and picked up two of her typed pages. Poring over them with intense concentration, she sat down in front of the desk, successfully blocking Margie from view, while the cameraman slowly turned toward his new, closer subject. TV lights came on, film rolled. Angel looked up, bathed in lights, an incredulous "what—me on television?" expression on her face, and then she looked down, resuming her intense scrutiny of Margie's work. Performances like this went on all day.

"The whole thing's getting away from us," said a top aide, descending from McGovern's penthouse suite. "I find I'm spending hours every day just trying to defend my job. I'm being pushed farther and farther from McGovern, more and more strangers seem to be taking over. What's going to happen to us all?"

Later that day, the staff once again gathered around

a television set to watch a rival withdraw. This time, it was Humphrey who stood at the Hotel Carillon, ashen-faced, his eyes brimming with tears, to announce in a slow, measured voice, "I will not permit my name to be entered in nomination at this convention. I am therefore releasing my delegates to vote as they wish." And that afternoon they pulled down the huge sign across the Carillon Hotel doorway which had read "Welcome Future President Humphrey."

Later in the day, maintaining my resolve to plan my own existence, and having once again not been offered a Service badge, I went over to the Fontainebleau and picked up my own press credentials for the Convention that night (which, with foresight, I had arranged for in the spring) and then went on to a party in the same hotel given by *Time* managing editor, Henry Grunwald. There, for the first time in Florida, I mingled with a roomful of people who seemed somewhat normal and appeared to be enjoying themselves. They even laughed occasionally, something I had forgotten how to do. Immediately, I felt better.

At one point in the evening, Mr. Grunwald suggested that the following morning I show some of my photographs to his picture editor at the Fontainebleau. I agreed and happily went off to my first night of the Convention, Tuesday, July 11—the Platform hearings.

And it was wonderful. This must be what conventions were all about—a huge hall, some 5,000 delegates, 8,000 newsmen, assorted individuals wearing tags of every description from "Media" to "Messenger," a constant parade of faces from the past, friends you'd known in the third grade, in the tenth grade, from the East, from the West, from everywhere.

Once in the Hall, I was, with the help of a friend, able to wangle a "Camera Stand" pass, which got me onto the Convention floor for the entire night instead of having to stand in line for a regular 15-minute revolving floor pass.

There was John Lindsay in the front row of seats, looking bemused, Kenneth Galbraith, Arthur Schlesinger, Marlo Thomas and Colonel Harlan Sanders from Kentucky Fried Chicken (whose company had paid $35,000 for the right to distribute its products in the Hall). There were hookers, working and non-working, Indians in full headdress, welfare mothers, Cornelia Wallace's mother, everyone.

The one upsetting thing that happened was the vote on the abortion plank. According to promise, the McGovern forces "released" their delegates to vote their consciences on this issue except that when it appeared that the plank might actually be accepted, they "unreleased" enough of them to ensure its defeat. Gloria Steinem was shaking and starting to cry. "You lied," she screamed at Gary. His standard quizzical-sincere expression came over his face. "I don't know what you're talking about," he said. "Oh, God," Gloria cried even louder, "I'm sick of this goddamn innocence."

First thing the next morning, I showed my photographs to *Time's* picture editor who offered to buy first-look rights until the end of the campaign and to send me to South Dakota with McGovern after the Convention. I was delighted and agreed to go if Frank approved.

When I returned to the press room, Miss Menopause

was having an anxiety attack. "I hear you were at the Convention last night," she said icily. "Tonight, you'll work in the trailer."

That was the night we formally won the Nomination to the accompaniment of tumultuous applause, shouts, and blaring recorded renditions of "Battle Hymn of the Republic." Since my important job had been to deliver piles of mimeographed nominating and seconding speeches to the delegates, I got a second night on the convention floor. Perhaps the actual Nomination was a bit of an anticlimax, but at least there was a definiteness about it. There would be no more speculation, no more "almosts," no more schemes to get the Nomination. We'd gotten it. All of us were now working for the Democratic nominee for President.

The best thing to take a picture of on Nomination night (since the candidate doesn't come to the Hall to accept his nomination until the following night) is the candidate's wife. This was a difficult thing to do.

It wasn't that Eleanor McGovern was inaccessible. She was extremely accessible, sitting in the first row of stage seats near the podium, looking radiant in a simple white dress. The problem was that there was something black draped across her, which obscured her left side from view. It was Henry Kimelman. Done up in a black jacket weighted down with several rows of medals, he was sitting inseparably close to the Senator's petite wife, leaning in front of her each time a flash bulb popped or television camera whirred. There were so many photographers around that night that poor Henry was forced to lean and straighten continually in an almost rhythmic fashion, giving him a somewhat jack-in-the-box appearance. With his black hair and tanned jutting features, Henry Kimelman made a strik-

126 □

ing figure, especially laden as he was with all those colorful medals. But I didn't really want a photograph of Henry Kimelman; what I wanted was Eleanor McGovern. In the end, I (and all the other photographers in the room) had to settle for half of each.

Afterward, there was a big victory party for "important staff" and fat cats at the Doral Starlight Roof, where everyone gathered red-eyed with exhaustion, but happy in an underplayed sort of way. Pierre was happy that he would get his job at the DNC. So would Jean Westwood. McGovern had now decided that, instead of appointing one Chairman, he would settle the argument with two Co-chairmen. Gordon was beaming and Kirby, whom I hadn't seen in days, showed the most tangible excitement of all. "We've done it," he shouted, jumping up and down and spilling his drink, "We've really done it!"

Seeing Gordon, Kirby, and several others in such good spirits Wednesday night, I was naturally surprised to pick up Thursday morning's *Miami Herald* and read about major changes in the McGovern staff. Frank Mankiewicz would remain National Political Director; Gary Hart, Campaign Manager in Charge of Field Operations; George Cunningham from the Senate staff would become Deputy Campaign Manager; Rick Stearns, Harold Himmelman, and Eli Segal, Regional Coordinators; John Holum would coordinate speech writing; Fred Dutton would now travel with the candidate while Gordon Weil stayed home in Washington as "Director of Research," and "Dick Dougherty would replace Kirby Jones as Press Secretary."

The heavies had won.

chapter 7

A Few Minor Staff Changes

It was Thursday, July 13, the day McGovern would announce his choice for Vice President. But it wouldn't be Ted Kennedy. The mystical moment of The Nomination had come, and the call had gone out to Hyannisport. No, said Kennedy. Sleep on it, said McGovern, and Kennedy had slept on it and again said no. So now speculation raged. Enough people apparently thought it might be Wisconsin Governor Pat Lucey, for there were red-and-blue-lettered tags already circulating through the Doral Hotel lobby—"McGovern–Lucey—Together We Win." But more bets were still on Connecticut's Senator Abe Ribicoff, Governor Reubin Askew of Florida, and Boston's Mayor Kevin White.

Frank was to make the announcement at a press conference in a main floor Conference Room at noon, which seemed rather early considering the number of candidates still in the running the night before. How could they boil it down from 14 to 1 in three hours? They couldn't. At noon, we stood packed together in the small room, television lights on, waiting.

At 12:30, I called upstairs to find out the length of the delay. Fifteen minutes, came the answer. Lights turned off. Fifteen minutes later, they switched on again. It was getting very hot. Another call upstairs. Another

☐ *129*

fifteen minutes. Lights off. Lights on. Announce a short delay, the seventeenth floor command post instructed. "Another delay," I announced. Lights off. And so it went until 1:30, when word came down to call off the press conference "until further notice."

"Must be getting a lot of rejections up there," a woman delegate laughed. I had felt slightly uneasy, hearing about the meeting held at 8 a.m. that morning, at which some twenty people had been asked to submit names of their four choices for Vice President. "I was shocked," said Ted Van Dyk later. "Before the California primary, I wrote the Senator a long memo about the necessity and procedures for organizing a selection committee to check out the candidates, and I naturally assumed it was being done. But instead, here we were, the day of the nomination, and Frank Mankiewicz is throwing out such suggestions as Walter Cronkite!"

Apparently, that meeting had broken up after suggestions had been narrowed down to six, including Sargent Shriver and Senator Thomas Eagleton from Missouri ". . . whose name," said Van Dyk, "kept coming up and just lying there." Gordon Weil was dispatched to check out rumors about a possible Eagleton drinking problem, and the next meeting was held at 11. At that one, Weil reported he could find no substance to the drinking rumors, and the list was narrowed further to Mayor Kevin White of Boston. McGovern phoned White, who said he'd be available. Stand by, said McGovern, I'll call you back in half an hour. Then what had happened, according to an aide present at all the meetings, was that McGovern called Kennedy to tell him about the White decision, to which Kennedy replied, "In that case, I'll have to reassess my own position. I'll call you back." What he had done in the way

130 ☐

of reassessing, said the aide, was to call Kenneth Galbraith, leader of the Massachusetts delegation and tell him to start a move on the floor to stop White's nomination.

Obviously, the choice of White didn't please Kennedy. White smacked of the old politics; he had originally been chairman of a delegate slate pledged to Muskie, not McGovern. In addition, being from the same state, White as Vice President could crowd Kennedy's political base. The White nominating petitions were already circulating on the Convention floor when Galbraith called McGovern to say his delegation would revolt if the choice were White. So much for Kevin White, who continued to wait by his telephone for the call that would never come.

Back at their hotels, Wilbur Mills and Leonard Woodcock, President of the United Auto Workers Union, whose names had been bandied about to appease business and labor, were waiting for calls, too. A spokesman for Woodcock phoned McGovern, reaching one of his aides. Woodcock, explained the caller, was stuck in his hotel suite with a number of important labor officials who were waiting to hear McGovern's decision; although Woodcock knew he wasn't the Vice Presidential choice, he desperately needed a face-saving call from McGovern.

But McGovern was disinclined to make the call. His aide, however, sympathizing with Woodcock's predicament, decided to do it on his own and phoned the bedroom of Woodcock's suite. There, in view, but out of earshot, of his peers, Leonard Woodcock was finally able to take his call from "McGovern."

Time was running out. There was a third meeting in McGovern's suite. Rick Stearns argued, as he had all along, for Larry O'Brien. But what about a nice Kennedy substitute, like brother-in-law Sargent Shriver, suggested Pierre. Call him, said McGovern. So Salinger did, but Shriver was in Moscow, unable to reach Miami in time for the nomination that night. So much for Shriver.

"I'm going to offer it to my friend, Gaylord" [Nelson, Senator from Wisconsin], said McGovern, reaching for the phone. But Gaylord Nelson said no, he'd promised his wife that he'd take the summer off. He, however, suggested Eagleton. So, in fact, had Kennedy and Senator Walter Mondale (Minnesota). McGovern turned to his secretary. "Get Tom Eagleton on the phone," he said. And then, he looked over at Ted Van Dyk and asked, "What do you think of Eagleton?"

"I think," said Van Dyk, "he's a nice guy, but I'm not quite sure he's up to the job."

"Is that so?" said McGovern.

And then the Eagleton call came through. "Tom," mumbled McGovern into the telephone, "I need a running mate—how about you?"

Waiting downstairs, everyone wondered about the delay. "It's because McGovern was so sure he'd get Kennedy he didn't have a backup choice," said a middle-level aide. "It's more than that," said an upper-middle aide who had attended the first meeting. "If Kennedy had accepted, there'd be real pandemonium up there. Only McGovern wanted him. Most of the staff was terrified that if Kennedy got on the ticket, he'd be too strong an influence on McGovern and he'd bring in all the pols and put a really good staff together that would threaten their positions. They felt the same way about Larry O'Brien, about any experienced politician, for that matter."

132 □

It was almost 4 o'clock when the press conference downstairs was hastily reassembled and Frank Mankiewicz walked in. He gave a long preamble about choosing a man with admirable qualities and so on, and then he paused, "That man," he said, "is Senator Thomas Eagleton of Missouri."

The classic "you could have heard a pin drop" expression applied at that moment. There was a kind of gasp from the reporters jammed in the hot, little room and then several seconds of silence. "Up to the last minute, we were strongly considering a Black and a woman," Gordon Weil told a reporter. A lot of bets had just been lost.

As I found out later, a lot of people had been lost, too. From the upper reaches of the Doral came rumors that Gordon Weil was quitting and going to Maine, because Fred Dutton was preempting his job. McGovern's secretary, Pat Donovan, as usual, was not around for McGovern's acceptance speech; she, too, had abruptly left Miami, angered that "the wrong people" (in this case Shirley MacLaine and Warren Beatty) were getting too close to McGovern. But Warren Beatty didn't remain as close as Pat feared. During the Vice Presidential selection meetings he was thrown out of McGovern's suite by Fred Dutton, and humiliated by being observed lurking around outside the door, had removed himself from town. Even Max Palevsky, one of the first big money men to support McGovern, had quit in a dispute over the Finance Chairmanship of the campaign and the choice of Eagleton. Palevsky, believing a McGovern-Kennedy ticket to be the only one which could beat Nixon, had been disgusted with the McGovern staff members who had argued against Kennedy for their own selfish reasons. And since California, he had been feuding with Henry Kimelman whom he considered another ineffectual McGovern yes man. In California, the word was that Kimelman had been let go in favor of Palevsky, but Kimelman had been "in from the start," always an important factor with McGovern, so he had now emerged as top finance dog. Palevsky took the 7:30 p.m. flight to Los Angeles.

I spent the rest of the afternoon typing several drafts of McGovern's acceptance speech and working on a biographical sketch of Eagleton; then, it was time to go to the Convention.

Tonight was the Convention's culminating night, floor passes were almost nonexistent, and newsmen were lining up for an hour just to get one 15-minute rotating floor pass. Everyone, of course, wanted to be on the floor when Kennedy spoke and McGovern accepted the nomination. I did too, but had to resign myself to watching it on TV when I saw how far down the pass list my name appeared. At that rate I wouldn't get on the floor until 3:00 a.m. As it turned out, with the balloting delays while the delegates offered such alternatives to Eagleton as Martha Mitchell, Archie Bunker, and Dr. Spock, McGovern ended up delivering his speech at 3:00 a.m. and I was on the floor.

Ted Kennedy spoke first. "Mr. Chairman, Delegates and fellow lettuce boycotters," he began, and the Hall exploded. Then he likened McGovern to the great Presidents in the Democratic tradition—Jefferson, Jackson, Wilson, Roosevelt. They had done wonderful things for the country, and—the resonant voice boomed out, "SO WILL GEORGE MCGOVERN. John Kennedy summoned every citizen to ask what he could do for his country—and SO WILL GEORGE MCGOVERN . . ."

134 □

McGovern good-naturedly accepted his loss of prime television time because of the balloting delay. "It took a long time," he said, "but we learned from watching the Republicans four years ago, as they selected their Vice Presidential nominee, that it pays to take a little more time." Later, he would agree that it would have paid to take even more.

And then he began.

"From secrecy and deception in high places—*come home, America.*"

"From the entrenchment of special privilege and tax favoritism—*come home, America.*

"From the prejudice of race and sex—*come home, America.*

"From the loneliness of the aging poor and the despair of the neglected sick—*come home, America.*

"Come home to the affirmation that we have a dream.

"Come home to the conviction that we can move our country forward.

"Come home to the belief that we can seek a newer world.

"For *this land is your land, this land is my land, from California to the New York island. From the red wood forest to the gulf stream waters, this land was made for you and me.*"*

The huge Hall came alive with an emotion of oneness: all my own feelings of discontent were blotted out by the music and singing. Through my camera's tele-

---

*"This Land Is Your Land," words and music by Woody Guthrie. TRO— © copyright 1956 and 1958, Ludlow Music, Inc., N.Y. Used by permission.

photo lens, I saw Frank Mankiewicz in the crowd, his furrowed face an enormous grin, his hands clasped to his chest, his eyes glistening. I, too, suddenly felt very lumpy-throated and very happy for everyone like Frank who had worked so hard for this moment.

To me, the speech was the high spot of the Campaign, and I believed it might be the springboard of a new mood of hope and unity not only within the Democratic Party but in the McGovern campaign itself.

People were still clapping and singing "We Shall Overcome" as an English journalist, Godfrey Hodgson, and I elbowed our way out of Convention Hall. Earlier in the evening, we had run into Yancey Martin, McGovern's Minorities Coordinator, who had invited us to Henry Kimelman's big victory party later that night (early morning as was the case). But when we arrived at the Doral's Starlight East Roof, there seemed to be a misunderstanding. Barring the entrance were two McGovern aides, rarely in evidence during the campaign so far. "It's for McGovern staff by invitation only," said one, pushing Godfrey aside. "I'm staff, and we've been invited by Yancey Martin," I said, feeling secure in that I had just spotted Yancey in the room.

I waved. Yancey stared. Godfrey waved. Yancey turned his back. "Well," said the doorstopper, looking enormously relieved that he could keep us out with impunity, "I guess he didn't invite you after all."

"Can you believe it?" asked the journalist. I told him I could. We stepped back from the line of people, most of whom were now being turned away, and resumed our conversation. Suddenly, Fred Dutton loomed up beside us, pulling at Godfrey's arm in midsentence. "Come on," he said, "I can sneak one person in." Godfrey hesitated, apparently weighing the party against my friendship. He determined he could probably have both.

There is something about having two people walk away from you in midconversation that can be slightly embarrassing, especially if someone you know is watching and naturally, someone was. *Washington Post* columnist Nick von Hoffman had been with us only a moment before and now, from the barstool directly behind me, I could feel his eyes boring into the back of my neck. Should I turn around and look as stupid as I felt or slink off to the ladies' room with a firm step that implied I had been headed there all along?

I didn't have my glasses on, though, and didn't know where the ladies' room was. I suspected, probably correctly, that I might look even more foolish should I now suddenly walk into a closet. I chose von Hoffman.

"That was really something," he laughed, ordering a double vodka. Six minutes later, Fred appeared at our elbows, wreathed in sheepish grins. "You didn't miss anything," he said. "The party's terrible."

"This is some People's Campaign," I snarled, hoping for some logical explanation of his very uncharacteristic behavior.

"Hell," said Fred, chuckling loudly and looking at Nick and then at me. "You never believed any of that stuff, did you? If you had any idea what was really going on in this campaign, you wouldn't want any part of it!"

He was holding his drink and laughing again but I feared he was speaking the only truth of the evening.

On Friday morning, after two hours sleep, I finally walked out of my steaming room at the "Ridge" and staggered off to the Doral. For once, I had actually seen the plane list for the flight back to Washington that afternoon and my name was on it.

I added my suitcase to the pile in the Doral lobby and went up to the press office to help pack the last of the files, releases, and office supplies. My head was in a carton when Angel cruised by. "I see your suitcase in the lobby, but there's no room on the plane," she said.

I removed my head from the carton. "It *is* on the list," I said wearily, in what was getting to be a re-hearsed script. "It's the fifth name on it, in fact, so there's got to be room unless we're traveling back by helicopter."

"Well, it's not on *my* list," said Angel, shoving it at me. And of course it wasn't. I finally realized something that if I'd had half a brain I would have figured out in February—that in a political campaign you should either have the very top job, such as be the Candidate or at least his Campaign Manager, or a bottom job that involves control of lists. There is little point in having any kind of job in the middle. Angel, Steve Robbins, and a couple of others had jobs solely involving lists, and lists can always be retyped to add or omit names by whim. Control of a list is Power.

On this particular morning, she and her counterpart, a man called John, had scratched names with an even heavier pencil than usual and the mezzanine floor rocked with cries of outrage from their victims. One girl from the Washington headquarters broke down and cried. "All the commercial flights are booked for the next two days," she sniffled noisily, "I've worked eighteen hours a day with no thanks at all, and I *know* my name was on the flight list. I don't have any money and if I'm stranded here for two days, I can't afford a hotel or food or anything." The tears came more copiously.

"There's always the bus," said John.

Someone from the scheduling office asked to see the list. He was refused. "But," said John again, "there's definitely no space for staff. You know the press comes first."

I reminded him that *most* of the staff, however, *was* on the plane. Angel suddenly looked interested. "But Kristi," she said, "the Senator only likes to travel with *certain* staff." Knowing McGovern, that seemed very hard to believe.

Ed O'Donnell, the young student coordinator whose efforts had contributed rather markedly to our victory in Miami had also been bumped. "It's the Peter Principle again," he said, "but this time, they're not going to get away with it."

They did for the moment, however, because now we were off to the final Convention event, the meeting of the Democratic National Committee at which McGovern would announce his new Co-Chairmen to replace the outgoing Chairman, Larry O'Brien.

Like the rest of us, Larry O'Brien had experienced a rather up and down career with the McGovern staff. Earlier in the spring, he had planned to leave the DNC job but McGovern had begged him to stay. So Larry had agreed and McGovern had then telephoned Frank Mankiewicz, who told him the staff objected (it would diminish their power if O'Brien was above them); so, McGovern said, "Sorry, Larry." Then, of course, McGovern realized he'd made an awful mistake and had again asked Larry to stay. This time Larry declined. Today, Friday, July 14, almost in the way of making polite conversation, McGovern had asked Larry one more time if there was any way he would change his mind and stay on. Larry said all right, he would. Then, suddenly, remembering his promise to Salinger and Westwood, McGovern once again said he couldn't. It was confusing at best.

The meeting of the National Committee at the Fontainebleau was short. Jean Westwood was nominated, seconded, and elected. Pierre Salinger was nominated and seconded. And then Charles Evers, a black Mississippi Mayor stood up and added a second name for nomination, that of black National Committeeman from New York, Basil Paterson. The Chairman asked whether either Salinger or Paterson wanted to withdraw their names. Neither did.

And then came a voice from the gold-curtained stage. "I just want to say," said George McGovern, "that I think these are both fine men and I would be pleased to have either one of them."

"I think Pierre just got the signal from George to jump out the window," said *Newsweek* correspondent John Lindsay.

Looking pale and speaking quickly, Pierre withdrew his name from the race.

"I want to thank Pierre Salinger . . ." droned McGovern.

"For taking that beautiful parachute dive," said Lindsay, beginning to laugh. "The McGovern boys did it again!"

Ed O'Donnell and I raced for the plane which was standing on the runway at the end of the Miami airport surrounded by Secret Service agents. A group of eight Washington-based staffers and volunteers sat forlornly in the shade under the plane's wing, hoping for seats on the flight. Ed and I stood in the baking sun and watched

John check off imaginary names from his list while Angel guarded the plane's door from an onslaught of the wrong people. As the next wave of correspondents and staff walked up to the steps, we crept up on John. Check. Check. Oops, here comes a fat cat and there's no fat cat name on the list. Hurriedly scribble fat cat name. Check. Scribble.

And then Dick Dougherty and McGovern arrived in a knot of reporters, ascended the steps and vanished inside the plane. Angel announced to the assembled volunteers that she would do a seat count. Very quickly, she reappeared at the plane's door and leaned out. "I've done a complete check," she said, in her most angelic way to the group under the wings, "and there isn't a single seat left." Sadly, the volunteers straggled off to the 28-hour bus.

But Ed and I refused to move. Instead, having realized the successes often wrought from McGovern staff tantrums, we threw a dual fit and demanded to see for ourselves. Just before they were rolled away, we marched up the stairs. But once on board, we were confronted with a problem—deciding just where to sit. There were 41 empty seats to choose from.

Back at the Washington headquarters, the Campaign Managers had a surprise in store for some of their devoted staffers who had toiled so hard and long in Miami. The envelopes containing our paychecks for the past 2 weeks were thicker than usual.

One 24-year-old boy who, at Frank's urgent request several months before, had moved his wife and small baby to Washington, looked stunned when he opened his. Probably got a bonus, I thought. Wordlessly, he handed me a mimeographed sheet of paper.

It was not addressed to anyone in particular, nor was it signed. It just began, "As you know, we are entering a 'slow' period in the campaign. Therefore, we are very sorry, but the enclosed check represents the last we can pay you for a while. When the campaign gets active again in the fall, we will be in touch with you." He was, in short, fired.

"I gave up a great job in Philadelphia," he said, gulping slightly. "What am I going to do now?" His voice rose as incredulity gave way to frustration. "I can't believe it," he cried, "we've won the damn nomination for them and now they dump us!"

"They're just clearing out the little unimportant people to make room for more heavies," muttered another staffer, a red-eyed girl who had also received the notice. Judging from facial expressions, it appeared that at least half the people in the room were now out of jobs. But there was nothing they could do about it. Gary and Frank were vacationing with Henry Kimelman in the Virgin Islands and, as usual, there was no one in charge.

Surprisingly, I hadn't gotten one. Maybe, I reasoned, after Frank had pressured me into giving up a top New York job, it would be too much even for this campaign to fire me now. It was hollow comfort.

chapter 8

The Short Flight
of Thomas Eagleton Seagull

On the hot, muggy morning of Monday, July 17, we took off for Rapid City, the closest we could get by jet to South Dakota's Black Hills. I looked forward to going West, far from the stultifying humidity of Miami and Washington and the gloom of the Campaign office. The flight on our chartered 727 was quiet—also a welcome change from the frantic pace of the weeks before. For one thing, besides Dick Dougherty and Fred Dutton, hardly any staff was along, only the Senator and Ila Pennington, Eleanor McGovern's twin sister (Mrs. McGovern was staying in Washington for a few days for a physical checkup), several McGovern children and grandchildren, the Secret Service, and about 40 newsmen.

For me, it was almost a vacation. For two glorious weeks, I wouldn't have to know McGovern's positions or schedule; I wouldn't have to type or Xerox, I couldn't be bumped off a plane. All I had to worry about was taking pictures for *Time* and looking at the campaign from a different perspective.

As the plane touched down at the Rapid City airport, we could see a huge sign supported by poles whipping in the wind above a crowd of several thousand. "Wambl Wan Kalinya, Kinyugato Po," it said in what I hoped was friendly Sioux. And while the crowd cheered, Indians danced and the Rapid City Rangers Band thumped out "Happy Days Are Here Again," McGovern thanked the crowd.

"I've come home because it seemed appropriate," he said, "home to the place where I have my roots and where I can restore my strength for the difficult months ahead." It was, as *Newsweek* correspondent Dick Stout pointed out, "your typical local-boy-makes-good atmosphere." And this boy had made very good. Standing there in the South Dakota wind, I was sure that in four months George McGovern would be President of the United States.

With "This Land is Your Land" ringing in our ears, we climbed into cars for the forty-mile ride by motorcade to Custer and the nearby resort area at Sylvan Lake where the McGoverns would spend the next two weeks resting and planning the coming campaign while we, the reporters, watched.

For the first time, I was to ride in a special photo car with four other photographers, two from Associated Press and two from United Press International. The air was at last clear and cool, the drive winding and long. I put my head down on a UPI camera bag and fell asleep.

In his car up ahead, McGovern did, too. Apparently, no one had bothered to inform him that the tiny town of Hill City had planned a huge "Welcome McGovern" celebration and that crowds waving signs, "Howdy George, you're in the heart of the hills," lined the streets to greet him. The Candidate was in a deep slumber as the motorcade raced through town.

All in all, it wasn't Hill City's very best day. Besides planning the celebration which nobody saw, local resi-

146 ☐

dents had also suspended an enormous "Welcome McGovern" sign across the main street. It was high but not quite high enough. A few minutes before the motorcade was due to arrive, a large Barber Transportation truck roared through town—and most unfortunately—also through the sign, leaving it in shreds on the street, where what life remained in it was immediately snuffed out by the wheels of the McGovern motorcade.

When I awoke, we had just arrived in the pine-covered hills of Custer State Park, where the McGoverns were disgorged in front of an unpretentious log cabin. Judging from a nearby sign, we didn't seem to be exactly in the center of things. The sign, with arrows pointing in different directions, offered only four choices: Custer—8 miles; Hill City—9 miles; Wind Cave—27 miles; and Deadwood City—57 miles.

McGovern took off his jacket and tie, and looking rather sleepy, stood on the cabin's steps while we took photographs. Then he retired for an afternoon of telephoning, on what turned out to be one of the area's few phones, while we wound our way back down the mountain and over to the Hi-Ho Motel, on the outskirts of the tiny town of Custer.

Since the Hi-Ho would be press headquarters during McGovern's 2-week stay in South Dakota, it was a matter of some concern that none of the rooms had phones. Fortunately, however, several had been installed in the pressroom, a regular bedroom on the motel's ground floor from which the bed had been removed and on the door a sign scotch-taped, saying "Press."

That evening we drove back up the mountain to the rustic Sylvan Lake Lodge for a buffalo feast in the main dining room, which featured dinner music, gaping onlookers, the local killer drink, the Hailstorm (a potent concoction of whiskey, syrup, and mint) and, of course, buffalo.

During the afternoon, the candidate had shucked off the East and now appeared at dinner in an open-necked shirt, silk ascot, and snappy suede jacket. He was followed by Dick Dougherty in hastily assembled Western—a blue jean jacket. McGovern, sitting with his family and Dougherty, gingerly sampled a Hailstorm, quietly replaced it with a dry martini. It was a relaxing evening, a very different atmosphere now that we had left behind most of the staff. After dinner, we drove along sparkling Sylvan Lake, lined by its majestic rock bluffs, then back down the mountain to Custer, a small town which looked like a movie set with swinging-door saloons, a tiny movie theater, and Indian craft stores lining its wide main street. There was beer to drink and pool to play at the sawdust-laden Gold Pan Saloon, featuring a naked picture of Goldie over the bar; then, it was time for the biggest event in town, the hanging of Fly Specked Billy.

Fly Specked Billy had been a local character in Old West days who had shot a man in a barroom brawl and resorted to such other antisocial antics as to have wound up hanged. Four times a week, they reenacted his hangin' in Custer, and tonight's performance drew a decidedly larger crowd than had the Presidential nominee's dinner appearance at the lodge.

The following morning was photo time—nothing exclusive, just appearances by the Candidate in local settings, beginning with Mt. Rushmore. It was a clear, bracing morning, and I was a nervous wreck, having sudden visions of stern-faced *Time* picture editors bending over endless rolls of completely blank film.

148 ☐

McGovern arrived wearing last night's dinner outfit and settled himself on a rock overlooking Mt. Rushmore, his profile set in line with the mountain's huge granite faces of former Presidents Washington, Jefferson, Theodore Roosevelt, and Lincoln, as reporters wisecracked about where in the group McGovern would fit. "The sculptor will comb the rocks forward to hide the bald spot," quipped one.

Everyone is clicking away furiously. This isn't the recreational photography I'm used to. This time, I can't hide a bad contact sheet. McGovern moves away, tourists press in, a hundred Instamatics blocking all view.

An aging Indian with feathers and what looks like a black Dynel wig is trotted out to tell McGovern that he'll be like a postage stamp, sticking with him that long. Quick—good (and only, it looks like) Indian shot. Switch to color camera. Click. We press inside local gift shop. Terrible light, constant motion, everyone pushing and shoving. I take a picture, by mistake, of Ila Pennington's ear. Take another of half an Indian bracelet which Candidate has just bought for Eleanor.

McGovern motions me to come upstairs and photograph him with local store owners. I do. All of them ask for copies while I panic that the film is no longer advancing. It is. I have decided that professional photographers have a bad life.

And then we were off to Hill City to reenact, not a hanging this time, but yesterday's unattended welcoming ceremony. McGovern spoke from a flatbed truck (fortunately, it wasn't snowing), the crowd loved him, and we headed back for the Sylvan Lake Lodge. The first day's shooting was over.

The Wednesday morning photo session featured George McGovern riding a horse through the ponderosa pines high into the Black Hills. This I looked forward to because one thing I can really do well is ride. But as I sadly discovered upon reaching the stable, the single-file lineup the Secret Service had arranged for us, headed by the Senator and followed by Secret Service agents, would, if I were riding, too, offer me only a selection of choice photographs of the preceding horse's tail. The only thing the photographers could do was run along beside the mounted candidate, 2 miles up the mountain and 2 miles down again—cameras clanking, panting, gasping.

At one point as I struggled to keep up, McGovern leaned over from his saddle. "You ought to be riding too," he said, "like Lady Godiva." "I can't," I wheezed, "my hair isn't long enough." "That would be even better," he said.

We returned to the stable where the candidate was greeted by the unhappy news that the AFL–CIO Executive Council had refused to endorse him, the first of several blows which would rock his vacation in the quiet Black Hills. This one was also to affect our immediate comfort, prompting McGovern to interrupt his vacation and return to Washington at 4 a.m. the following morning, Thursday, July 20, to vote on a key labor issue, the minimum wage bill. We would return to South Dakota on Friday.

After calling the editor at *Time* who suggested I stay with McGovern for the round-trip flight, I pounced on Dick Dougherty to add my name to the list. I watched him write it down; it was the sixth one—right after Bill Greider of *The Washington Post*, just before Dick Stout of *Newsweek*. It was important, I'd found, to remember details such as these.

That night, McGovern celebrated his fiftieth birthday with a big party at the lodge for some 75 South Dakota friends, his small staff, and the press. Again we had buffalo, in a somewhat different form, and a big, white birthday cake shaped like the White House and surrounded by tiny flags from 36 states. Thirty six? Someone scurried off to the kitchen for more flags while I rushed up to take a flash picture of McGovern as he sliced off the cake's roof. "I know that's what George Meany thought would happen all along if I got in," he laughed.

It was only a few hours later, 3 a.m., when I dragged myself out of my comfortable room at the Hi-Ho and into Bill Greider's car for the hour's drive to Rapid City. We all got on the plane, television lights trained on McGovern as he arrived in the darkness and climbed up the plane's steps, looking as tired as we felt. I was very sorry to leave the clear air and happy atmosphere of South Dakota, but I thought, it was only for a day.

Arriving in Washington at 8 in the morning was a culture shock. The entire East Coast was in a state of near emergency due to an air pollution inversion. The temperature hovered near 100°, the sky was a thick gray, no wind stirred. "Don't take a deep breath," the radio station warned, but you couldn't if you tried. There seemed to be no air to breathe, just wet, gray moisture. After McGovern voted at the Senate, we went to a press conference in the Senate Office Building where he announced his latest appointment— Larry O'Brien would now become National Campaign Chairman. After McGovern had spoken, he and Tom Eagleton flanked O'Brien and all of them smiled for the photographers. The whole display produced a feeling of great unity, but I thought it strange that during this performance on stage, Mankiewicz and Hart were almost skulking at the fringes of the room.

Back at the office, everyone was packing for the move to our new K Street headquarters. Cartons covered the floor—mounds of outdated press releases, bumper stickers, staplers, rolls of Scotch tape and old stationery were being sorted out by perspiring volunteers.

Out of this confusion Marion Pearlman's secretary suddenly appeared hurriedly dispensing envelopes. One came in my direction and I tore it open with trembling fingers, knowing what it would say, "As you know, we are entering a 'slow' period . . . Therefore, this is your last check . . ." They had added more victims to their list.

But my last day in the First Street headquarters was not yet complete. On arriving in Washington, *Time* had informed me that one of their top staff photographers would join me in South Dakota for the following week. I had immediately added his name to the plane list, which Dick Dougherty had placed in the capable hands of Steve Robbins.

Now, several hours later, Robbins had completed his juggling act. He loomed up behind me. "I've bumped that *Time* photographer," he said in his matter-of-fact tone. "The plane's full and we can't take two people from the same magazine, and we have too many staff."

"That's ridiculous," I pointed out. "You have five members from the same organization in each TV film crew, two photographers and a reporter from UPI, two photographers and a reporter from AP . . ."

"That's the way it is," Robbins said smugly. I protested again.

"O. K., if you don't like it, then you're bumped too," he said.

I felt dizzy with helpless rage. "Why me?" I yelled.

"Because," he smiled now, "who else can I bump? A lot of staff are going out to South Dakota this time for strategy meetings. We're taking a Washington tennis pro to play with the Senator, and Mary McGovern's boy friend, and a couple of husbands and wives, lots of extra people. I have to bump someone. "Bump the tennis pro," I suggested, "I'll play tennis with George."

Robbins looked weary. "Joe Grandmaison wants to come out this time," he said. "If I bump him and he has to take a commercial flight, you'll hear a temper tantrum you won't believe. No one wants that. But if I bump you, well, there's not a damn thing you can do. And nothing that other *Time* photographer can do either. You don't have anyone protecting you."

I had never bothered Frank with trivia. Even if I'd wanted to, it would have been impossible because of the constant buffer of telephones he maintained between himself and anyone who might possibly burden him with a problem. But this time I did. As he sat in his office in an unguarded moment, talking to his assistant, Pat Broun, I walked in and in a very detached way told him what I had seen happening in the campaign: the staff viciousness, the constant plotting and the incompetence it caused, the volunteers who were forced to travel 28 hours by bus from Miami while a half-empty plane returned to Washington, the constant unnecessary bumping of people from their seats, the impossibility of getting the schedule, the notices terminating salaries sent out without warning, the elitism of a staff which was antagonizing everyone around

□ *153*

them, and the fact that if all this continued it, would end up really hurting only one person, but hurting him badly. That person was George McGovern.

Frank lifted his eyebrows. He looked very tired, his face etched with dark shadows. "It can't be," he said. "It just can't be."

And off he rushed to catch the McGovern plane for South Dakota with its important load of tantrum-prone staffers, tennis pros, and boy friends. Even Mary McGovern's Newfoundland retriever, Atticus, had a seat. The *Time* photographer and I traveled to Dulles Field an hour from Washington, to catch a commercial flight to Denver, where we waited a couple of hours for another flight to Rapid City, where we rented a car, and in a blinding rain and hail storm, drove another hour and a half to the Hi-Ho Motel, pulling in at 2:20 a.m., a pleasant 11-hour journey courtesy of that scheduling wizard, Robbins.

With the influx of staff, the atmosphere in the Black Hills changed. Rumors, absent earlier in the week, were being leaked to the press by those most anxious to make them true. Larry O'Brien, said one, would be only a figurehead with no real power—no threat to anyone on the McGovern staff. Fortunately, most of the newly arrived staff spent their time at meetings, while my days were a blur of photographs and attempted photographs: McGovern playing tennis with the pro, McGovern in his cabin, McGovern singing in the lodge after dinner to the accompaniment of John Holum's 12-string guitar, McGovern and his wife (who had come out on the Friday flight) watching the sunset over Sylvan Lake.

McGovern berated the planters of the O'Brien rumor and begged the staff to stop the leaks by "highly placed aides." Before the afternoon was over, of course, the exact phrasing of his request to *stop* the leaks was leaked to UPI. Most of the staff returned to Washington after the Saturday strategy meeting, but Jean Westwood stayed on and asked me to meet with her. With a correspondent from the *Chicago Tribune*, we sat on the terrace while she outlined her plans for the Democratic National Committee, her intentions of traveling around the country on speaking engagements, and her hopes for her staff. Would I like to be her press secretary?

Since I had always particularly liked Jean Westwood and believed her to be about the only person in the campaign genuinely interested in the status of women, I quickly said yes, wondering at the same time, however, what this would do to my reputation. Would everyone now add *her* to my list of lovers?

Tom Eagleton and his wife arrived the following night, and on Tuesday morning, July 25, those of us who remained in the Black Hills assembled in a bare log cabin in the pines for his press conference. It was a cool, cloudy day, and the damp cabin reminded me of the sort of place you were sent to string beads or mold animal figures in clay on a bad day at summer camp.

It would be just a routine press conference during which, presumably, Senator Eagleton would announce the thrust of his campaign (to provide as great a contrast as possible to Spiro Agnew) and McGovern would talk about his plans for meshing the organizations of the two campaigns. I was mainly interested because it would be my first chance to photograph the McGoverns and Eagletons together.

There was a long delay while we milled around the room drinking coffee and then they came in—McGovern and Eagleton in open-necked shirts and sports jackets, Eagleton's an exceedingly loud, checked variety, the two wives in conservative prints. The four of them stood dutifully around the wooden podium with its jagged arms of microphones while we took pictures. Then McGovern introduced his running mate. Eagleton stood up to speak, McGovern sat down to one side, the two wives together on the other. Good. A chance to take Eleanor McGovern with Barbara Eagleton, who appeared to be wearing a Spiro Agnew watch.

I hadn't been paying much attention to Eagleton's opening remarks but now something made me listen. "There have been some rumors circulating as to my health," he was saying. "On three occasions in my life, I have voluntarily gone into hospitals as a result of nervous exhaustion and fatigue . . ."

I looked at Barbara Eagleton. Her hands were clasped on her lap, her eyes somewhat glassy. Eleanor McGovern reached over and squeezed her hand. George McGovern's mouth was set in a tight line and Dick Dougherty, standing off to the side in his blue jean jacket, was unconsciously, but literally, wringing his hands.

It got worse and worse. Eagleton, now perspiring heavily, proceeded to outline details of three hospitalizations for periods ranging from 4 days to 4 weeks.

There was a long, rather painful period of questions during which he admitted also to having had psychiatric help and electric shock treatments. And then McGovern spoke.

"If I had known every detail that he [Eagleton] discussed with me this morning, which is exactly what he has just told you here now, he would still have been my choice for the Vice Presidency of the United States

. . . I can't think of anybody in the Senate that would have been any greater credit to the ticket than Tom Eagleton. And that's the way I feel."

I was glad he felt that way. So far in the campaign, there had been some painful examples on everyone's part of somewhat less than total commitment to others. But now, I thought, McGovern had shown guts, decency, and a strength of spirit. The press conference ended and the foursome walked out stiffly to a waiting car which would whisk Thomas Eagleton Seagull to the airport for his last flight on the McGovern campaign.

Newsmen scrambled down the hill to the few available telephones, TV correspondents raced to the airport with film, and a horde of others descended on their typewriters. "A gutsy performance," said Fred Dutton. "It could turn into a plus," said Bill Dougherty, Lieutenant Governor of South Dakota. "I wouldn't exactly call it a plus," said Frank.

For the first time in our 8 days in the Black Hills, the press had a real story, but from the campaign's standpoint it couldn't have come at a worse time. Here were some 40 newsmen cooped up in a remote area with a Presidential Candidate about whom they were forced to keep writing. But with limited access to television, telephones, and newspapers (which normally arrived several days late), they could do little but feed on information from each other. We now entered a period of intense speculation, what today's revelation would do to the Campaign and whether, and if so, when, Tom Eagleton might go the way of Pierre Salinger, Gordon Weil and Kirby Jones.

Tuesday's story was Eagleton's mental health news, but for Wednesday, they had nothing yet but conjecture. Associated Press theorized that Eagleton might soon be dropped, prompting McGovern to make a statement dutifully carried down to the Hi-Ho Motel press room by Dick Dougherty, who read in measured tones, "The Senator has said today that he is one thousand percent behind Tom Eagleton and has no intention of dropping him from the ticket." Mistake. McGovern should certainly have realized by this time that 1,000 wasn't his best number. Now the press had something for Wednesday—the 1,000 percent story. At the same time, due to a faulty transmission process, telegrams addressed to McGovern at the lodge were coming in by mistake over the pressroom AP ticker, allowing all of us to read reactions and opinions which should have been kept strictly private.

"Since you have conceded election to Nixon by selection of psychotic," read one, "I would like refund of money contributed when you were a viable candidate."

Later that afternoon, Dougherty and Dutton returned to the press room. "The position as of now," Dougherty reiterated, stressing the *now*, "is to stick with Senator Eagleton." "We're getting an awful lot of pressure from the other side," said Dutton. "I'd say the situation right now is at a slow boil." Like two circus clowns whose tent had caught fire, they alternated between facing the gravity of the situation and trying to entertain the crowd.

This was my chance, I decided, to give Fred Dutton my 2-minute version of why we had no choice but to keep Eagleton and how McGovern could turn a bad situation into a good one by recalling American history, reminding people that the whole country was built on the concept of starting over, of judging a man, not on what he has been, but on what he has become. So Eagleton had been sick and had had the good sense to see

158 □

a doctor and get well, something a lot of others might be wise to do themselves.

Fred shook his head. "That won't work," he said. "The country just doesn't understand mental health."

And it seemed that he was right. Already the jokes were starting, "It's a great ticket, a Commie and a kook."

"Question: How do you tell McGovern's Secret Service agents from Eagleton's?"

"Answer: Eagleton's wear white coats."

On Thursday, an uptight atmosphere was taking hold. McGovern canceled a scheduled press conference and publicly issued an ultimatum to the staff, in Washington and Custer, to keep their mouths shut on the subject of Eagleton. Keep their mouths shut but let the pressure build up so Eagleton would come to "the appropriate conclusion." Everyone began to speak more openly about the Eagleton "disaster." Sissy Farenthold and Queens County Democratic leader, Matt Troy, denounced him, the latter going so far as to say he had "been promised by Dick Dougherty that Eagleton would be off the ticket in 24 hours." "It's a lie," said Dougherty, "I haven't spoken to Matt Troy since he left here last weekend."

Dutton and Dougherty pushed to drop Eagleton quickly; Gary and Frank, who had been against the press conference announcement to begin with, equivocated, while behind the scenes, Larry O'Brien rushed to sound out important politicians. Los Angeles industrialist Miles Rubin quietly assured jittery fat cats that Eagleton's days were numbered, and Joseph Califano, Chief Counsel for the Democratic National Committee, checked procedures for picking a new Vice Presidential nominee.

Out on the West Coast, however, Eagleton was missing the message. Instead, he was picking up support from the polls and such Party Regulars as Chicago's Mayor Daley and Philadelphia Democratic Committee Chairman Peter Camiel. The already yawning abyss between the Party Regulars and the McGovern campaign could now only be widened by a backstage move to drop Eagleton.

And then columnist Jack Anderson got into the act. He had it from a reliable source that Eagleton had been arrested for drunken driving in Missouri (a charge he later couldn't back up), adding another problem for McGovern. Now any attempt by McGovern's staff to get Eagleton's medical records (which had been promised but not delivered) would be regarded as further dumping on a downed duck. And now also, we were stuck in a timing twilight zone. If we were going to do it at all, we should have dropped Eagleton immediately, which would have looked decisive. Having failed to do that, we now had to wait longer, to at least give the impression of great deliberation and thought going into the choice of successor.

Meanwhile, reactions from around the country kept coming in on the pressroom telephones and the AP wire. By late Thursday, the mood seemed to be turning for the first time. Phone calls were running slightly pro-Eagleton, the telegrams about half and half. Since it had been decided to let public pressure force Eagleton off the ticket, this wasn't the happiest development. But it didn't last long. Coming back from a barbecue that night, a group of us met Dick Dougherty in the driveway of the Hi-Ho Motel. Looking preoccupied and a bit bulkier than usual, he quickly walked off toward his car. But he made a crunchy noise doing it, a

160 □

bit like one of those crispy cereal commercials. It was only when we entered the pressroom and saw that the AP ticker had been denuded of its rolls of wire copy did we suspect that possibly Dougherty had been wearing some of the most recent Eagleton comments. The next morning McGovern passed down the word—telegrams were running two to one against Eagleton.

Thursday afternoon, we went to Custer's local movie theater for a private screening of "The Candidate," a film about a trusting young man who turns into a conniving politician. The McGoverns, sitting in the dark theater eating popcorn, laughed particularly loudly when one character in the film, the Campaign Manager, instructed the Press Secretary to "get all the reporters on the press bus and drive them over the nearest cliff."

Meanwhile, out on the West Coast, Eagleton talked happily about the encouragement he was getting from party leaders, and about his enthusiastic Hawaiian reception. It was time to send him a stronger message and it took the form of Jules Witcover, correspondent for the *Los Angeles Times*, who happened to have written a book about the Vice Presidency and had once discussed it with McGovern. Jules was in the press room with *Time*'s Dean Fischer and *Newsweek*'s Dick Stout when a call came through from the candidate. Would Mr. Witcover care to have a drink at the Senator's cabin at 6 p.m. and talk about the Vice Presidency? He would. And did.

In his small log cabin, McGovern explained his feelings. He was talking to Witcover for the purpose of a story, but one which he did not want attributed to him. Tom Eagleton was out of touch, isolated, said McGovern, but perhaps if a newspaper article apprised him of what was going on, he'd get the message and do the right thing. Eagleton, reading Witcover's story the next morning in San Francisco, might then finally pick up a couple of hints that McGovern's 1,000 percent support was down just a bit—to maybe 2 percent.

The whole thing, said McGovern, had been terrible luck, not really his fault. He had always counted on Kennedy, had believed that when the moment of the actual Nomination came, Kennedy would be swept up. Then the fact that the margin in California hadn't been as big as expected meant he'd had to spend more time on the New York primary. Finally, the California challenge had cost him the time in late June that he'd planned to deliberate about the Vice President. He hadn't known Eagleton very well but Senators Mondale, Nelson, and Kennedy had all recommended him. None of them had known about his medical history. How could he? Nor, when he found out, had he realized it would cause such a flap. But now the public and political reaction was so severe that Eagleton had to go. He was already considering replacements.

That night as Witcover pounded out his story back at the Hi-Ho, McGovern table-hopped at dinner with the rest of the reporters at the Sylvan Lake Lodge. The Eagleton thing had ruined his vacation, he said, but he'd kept hoping for the best. Now it was up to Eagleton to realize that if public opinion was against him, he should withdraw. If Eagleton didn't get the message from the *Los Angeles Times,* maybe the combined forces of *Time, Newsweek,* AP, UPI, *The New York Times, The Washington Post,* the *Chicago Tribune,* the *Wall Street Journal, Knight Newspapers,* and CBS could make it sink in.

But Eagleton still didn't get the message. The next

162 ☐

morning, Saturday, July 29, after talking to McGovern by phone, he was still cheerily telling newsmen, "All he [McGovern] said was, I'm for you 1,000 percent . . . The way this has turned around, I'm a distinct plus to the ticket. I'm going to stay on the ticket. That's my firm, irrevocable intent."

Meanwhile, back in South Dakota, McGovern was winding up his vacation in what had become known as the Bleak Hills. "Senator Eagleton and I had a lengthy conversation this morning," he said in a statement issued by Dick Dougherty, "and I assured him I am still backing him as Vice Presidential nominee of the party. Senator Eagleton and I have agreed to meet Monday evening for a mutual assessment. Rumors and reports of any decision having been made on this question are misleading." Where did that leave Jules Witcover?

So, with McGovern's approval, Tom Eagleton took his story, a modified Checkers number, to CBS's *Face the Nation*. Half an hour later, Jean Westwood and Basil Paterson took McGovern's story to NBC's *Meet the Press*. "It would be the noble thing for Tom Eagleton to resign," said Mrs. Westwood.

And then, finally, it was over. In an anticlimactic meeting in Washington the following evening, Monday, July 31, McGovern accepted Eagleton's resignation. Why all the deceit? everyone asked. Why hadn't McGovern handled the situation like a Kennedy and told Eagleton, "You've got so many hours to get off the ticket, now do it"?

The reason may be that McGovern was caught completely off guard. As he admitted himself, he had believed the nomination to be a mystical event; that, once getting, it he could have anything he wanted. Finally, he had gotten it, and then, wham, before he could even contemplate what it was he had actually won, something was threatening to take it all away. And, more than anyone else, George McGovern believed his Good Guy image, which he had to square with his behavior. He felt deeply concerned about Eagleton as a person and how he would be affected, but naturally his greatest concern had to be the effect of Eagleton on his own candidacy and on the Democratic Party. From the time of his childhood as the minister's son, George McGovern had always believed he was telling the truth. The most important thing to him was his integrity, even if he had to play games with himself to preserve it.

chapter 9

Playing Out a Bad Hand

I returned to New York to unpack, repack, and hopefully arrange for a place to live for the next three
months in Washington, and so did not have to witness
at close hand the humiliating week-long public search
for Eagleton's replacement.

In my life, at least, one thing went right. Barbara
Howar, a friend summering in Long Island, offered me
the use of her comfortable Georgetown town house
until the November election. For the first time since I
joined the campaign, I would have a permanent bed.

I arrived back in Washington two days after Sargent
Shriver had enthusiastically agreed to join the ticket,
and immediately called the DNC and asked for Jean
Westwood.

There was a long silence, and the sound of rattling
pages on the other end of the phone. And then an un-
familiar voice came back. "I'm sorry," it said, "there's
no one by that name here."

"Jean Westwood," I said again enunciating the three
syllables. "She's your boss, she's the Chairman of the
Democratic National Committee."

"Oh," said the voice again. More rattling. "Well, she
doesn't seem to be listed."

The campaign was off to a great start.

I spent the next morning unpacking and calling friends at headquarters, none of whom appeared to work there anymore, Jean Westwood, who still wasn't listed, and Mother.

"That was some Convention, dear," said Mother.

"I thought it was terrific," I shot back defensively. "McGovern's acceptance speech was beautiful."

"Well, no one heard the speech at three o'clock in the morning," she went on, "but we did see something I'm afraid you didn't—television coverage of the whole Convention. McGovern's supporters came across as awfully radical. There was hardly a normal looking person in that Hall."

Her assessment coincided, unfortunately, with the opinion of the Yankelovich poll which determined that McGovern's image in recent weeks had slipped from "strong liberal" to "weak radical."

Just as discouraging, another poll taken six days after Eagletons mental health announcement, found that 61% of those sampled thought he should stay on the ticket against 29% who thought he should be dropped. Worse was the fact that most of those who thought Eagleton should be dropped intended to vote for President Nixon anyway.

Failing to make any human contact at the DNC office at the Watergate or at our new campaign office on K Street, I took a cab over to the Sheraton Park Hotel where the Democratic National Committee was meeting that evening to formally name Shriver as McGovern's newest running mate. Of course, the whole thing could have been done in the afternoon, but since NBC was planning to cover the evening session live, complete with David Brinkley and John Chancellor in an anchor booth and the four Convention floor reporters cruising about among the delegates, the Democrats decided to put on a whole production. The little Sheraton ballroom was done up like a miniature Convention floor with lots of red, white, and blue crepe paper, state standards, life-sized portraits of past Democratic Presidents, floor passes, and a microphone-laden podium facing cordoned-off sections of the floor for delegates, observers, and press.

With a canned version of "Bridge over Troubled Waters" ringing over the hall, the mini-convention began. Up on the podium, almost frozen in their positions and exuding unity, sat Humphrey, Kennedy, Muskie, Jackson, Eagleton, and Larry O'Brien. Why O'Brien kept bouncing back no one could figure out. Besides playing the mouse in McGovern's continual game of cat and mouse, he had also reportedly been given the Kevin White treatment in the most current game of "Let's pick a V. P." Stand by, Larry, McGovern had told him the week before while he wound his way down his list of Eagleton replacements, you're next in line if Muskie turns it down. Muskie had turned it down, but somehow Shriver had gotten ahead in line and hopefully, by now, Larry had stopped waiting for his call.

Despite a very good speech by McGovern (a mini-version of the Miami Convention's Come Home America), the mood of the evening was more like a wake than a christening. The body was in full view on stage. There were eulogies—what a wonderful man the deceased had been, what a noble thing he'd done in dying just when he did—and all the while, Thomas Eagleton sat there perspiring, his hand rigidly grasping the side of his chair, his mouth stuck in a fixed, embalmed smile.

Sargent Shriver, looking tan and handsome in a dark suit, surrounded by his vibrant wife, Eunice, and three beautiful children, finally closed the coffin. He would carry on for the deceased. "I'm not embarrassed to be McGovern's seventh choice for Vice President," he said. "We Democrats may be short of money but we're not short of talent. Pity Mr. Nixon . . . his first and only choice was Spiro Agnew!" The "up" mood was back. I felt momentarily hopeful again.

Momentarily. Listening to the music, watching the State standards bouncing up and down, and the photographers scurrying to the podium, I suddenly remembered that I'd seen all this before. This was a nice little Convention. The only trouble was it was a nice little *second* Convention. When you're the Candidate for President, you're supposed to do it right the *first* time.

And suddenly, I realized the obvious: the McGovern campaign was over. Later, the experts would say it had gone wrong in California in June with Humphrey's vicious attacks on McGovern's proposals for welfare and defense. Others would say it went wrong at the Convention or in South Dakota in July with the Eagleton affair, still others would say the last straw came in Washington in October with Henry Kissinger's announcement that "peace is at hand." But they were all a few years off. The campaign hadn't gone wrong. It was never there. And it was never there because it had never really been McGovern's campaign; it was a Kennedy replacement. It was the wrong year and McGovern was the wrong man.

The campaign was doomed from the start—from its inception during the 1968 Democratic National Convention in Chicago. There, McGovern had a moment of glory and attention when he filled in for the dead Robert Kennedy as a possible alternative to Humphrey. He got the sentimental vote of Bobby's California delegation and the support of former Kennedy people like Pierre Salinger and Roosevelt Grier—just long enough for him to be fatally bitten by the Presidential bug. But he was only *filling in* for Bobby and *standing in* for Ted. It was always clearly understood that all votes for McGovern were reserved for Ted Kennedy should he be persuaded to run.

McGovern's Presidential effort began as a Kennedy shadow and the shadow didn't shrink. He tried to surround himself with people who had worked for the Kennedys—Frank Mankiewicz, Pierre Salinger, Fred Dutton, Gary Hart, and others—who in turn brought in still more, swelling the Kennedy ranks. During the primaries, McGovern was never able to completely shake off his stalking horse image. Instead, his need for Kennedy grew. When Bobby's widow, Ethel, appeared in Florida during that primary, a tremendous fuss ensued over whether she would or wouldn't endorse McGovern. She didn't. But her daughter, Kathleen, did, and became a featured attraction on the McGovern traveling campaign. On the radio, tapes of Bobby Kennedy's voice periodically reminded anyone who might have forgotten, that although Ted Kennedy hadn't come through for McGovern, another Kennedy had thought the South Dakota Senator pretty terrific. As he neared the Nomination, McGovern increasingly realized his need for a Kennedy on the ticket; by the time of the California primary, he constantly attached himself to the Kennedy image by keeping alive the rumor that Kennedy would come aboard as Vice President.

McGovern misjudged Kennedy's vague not "yes," not "no" answers. He thought Kennedy was more like him, just keeping flexible, not getting locked in, and

□ *171*

that with a changing situation (winning the Nomination) his no could just as easily wind up yes. McGovern never saw that his campaign was a Kennedy copy and that, like many copies, it just missed.

By picking men by virtue of their Kennedy connections, he ended up with political innocents, talented men cast out of their proper roles. Frank Mankiewicz and Pierre Salinger, former Press Secretaries, were turned into National Political Director and National Political Coordinator; Gary Hart, a local Kennedy worker in the Rocky Mountain States, into Campaign Manager.

The Kennedy influence was crippling. It prevented people from lending their expertise from past campaigns to George McGovern. Instead, they just kept wishing it were the other campaign.

Unlike other campaigns where some sort of devotion to the candidate is the norm, many of McGovern's supporters seemed to be accepting him as the next best thing. Most of them were more interested in an issue, peace, or a process, party reform. There really never were any "McGovernites."

In the end the Kennedy influence destroyed McGovern. If he hadn't so tenaciously held out for Kennedy, he would have looked for a running mate sometime before the very last day of the Convention; had he not then let Kennedy dissuade him from his choice of Kevin White nor had he heeded Kennedy's suggestion of Eagleton, we would not now have been walking out of a mini-convention, culminating months of hope for a Kennedy on the ticket with instead, a seventh choice Kennedy substitute, the brother-in-law. In a sense, Ted Kennedy, who had been so sought after to save the ticket had inadvertently destroyed it.

The next morning I walked from Georgetown to look for Jean Westwood at the sprawling apartment, office, hotel complex known as the Watergate. Up on its sixth floor, the headquarters of the DNC was a quiet, thickly carpeted operation, in which, although the switchboard didn't know it yet, Jean Westwood had an office. Her male secretary, formerly assistant to the assistant scheduler during several primaries, looked up nervously. "Mrs. Westwood is busy," he said, glancing over his shoulder at a closed door, "but there are no jobs here." He was right.

Eventually, out came Alan Barons, another assistant, who told me, with obvious embarrassment, that in South Dakota when Jean Westwood had offered me the job, she hadn't realized the DNC had no money. I could work for her as a volunteer only—if I needed salary no one there could pay it.

I hadn't seen any salary for three weeks, nor the $700 now owed me in expenses, and my heart was therefore not in an appropriately volunteer-oriented mood to accept this particular offer. I mumbled something to Barons about being surprised—which I no longer was—and walked over to 1910 K Street, our new campaign office about a mile away.

The new headquarters was conveniently located, near the good restaurants and shops and next to a large parking lot, and it was filled with such previously unknown luxuries as two elevators and 16 bathrooms. Where we had been crowded before, offices at K Street were vast to the point of emptiness. Although, as usual, furniture was scarce, living people were scarcer and many of the familiar faces were gone from the press room. Miss Menopause now ruled over Margie, the political science major, and a motley collection of newly

□ 173

hireds. In an adjoining room, Kirby Jones, having inherited the vacant Deputy Press Secretary title, sat staring out the window laughing at a private joke, and in the office next to him sat Ed O'Donnell, wearing a bemused expression and doodling on a yellow-lined pad.

"It's a disaster," he said, "everything's that's been under the surface is coming out. We're right back where we were at the beginning." His beginning had been 2 years before mine. In November 1970, while on a Rockefeller Fellowship to Harvard, he had come to the tiny McGovern campaign office, then located in a town house on Maryland Avenue and had had lunch with Rick Stearns, Jeff Smith, and Gary Hart to discuss doing some work for McGovern on campuses. Stearns and Smith had been very seriously discussing their opinions of polling techniques, Ed recalled, when suddenly Gary Hart, in sunglasses and cowboy boots, had burst out laughing and announced that his opinion was he wanted a second piece of cake and another bottle of beer. "Gary wasn't a typical politician," said Ed. "He seemed interested in people, not all the ego stuff. He was the main reason I decided to join the campaign."

It had been a happy atmosphere for several months and then the intrigue had begun, starting in McGovern's own office by closest confidants, his secretary, Pat Donovan, and Senate aide, George Cunningham. "Both of them constantly told McGovern about the incompetence of the rest of his staff," Ed remembered. "They turned him into a henpecked man, forced to waste time every day asking one staff member to verify the most recent accusations against another. It diffused his energies and made him mistrust his staff and naturally lots of them quit. Those who stayed were never delegated any responsibility so when McGovern was away, no one else ever had any authority."

But McGovern himself was equally the target of their jealousy. From the very beginning, there had been a battle between the Senate staff and the small campaign staff, said one long-time observer, ". . . because those who worked for McGovern in the Senate office really didn't want him to run for President. If he became the Presidential Candidate, the campaign office would take over from the Senate office and he would then be surrounded by pros with wider vision than his narrow-minded South Dakota aides, who feared, of course, that they'd be cut out."

The night McGovern announced his candidacy, George Cunningham reportedly locked the Senate office at 5 p.m. so no telephone calls or telegrams could get through, so angering several campaign staff members that they tried to kick in the door.

So why didn't McGovern do something about his staff? Lots of people asked that very question, but George McGovern always had the same answer for everyone who complained. "Give them another chance."

And McGovern was always giving second chances, and even third and fourth, possibly because his religious background helped him believe in redemption and also because he valued a particular kind of political loyalty over competence. If you'd been with him from the start, despite any number of screwups on your part, chances were awfully good you'd still be there at the end. And if you hadn't, chances were equally good you would find yourself slowly eased out. McGovern never totally trusted anyone who seemed independent, had more experience than he did, or who had been previously committed to someone else, and that included O'Brien, Salinger, Dutton, Mankiewicz, and Van Dyk.

Gary Hart, however by the nature of his basically spear-carrying role for Bobby Kennedy in '68, was clean. He did what he was told and was there from the start.

While McGovern had been winning the primaries and then the Nomination, much of the under-the-surface tension had been covered up while those with the most to gain silently maneuvered to assure their positions in the new structure of the post-Convention campaign. But now it was the winners who felt bitter. They had fought and won, but suddenly their victory had been wrenched from them by Tom Eagleton, Gordon Weil, who had checked out Eagleton, and George McGovern, who had picked Eagleton in the first place.

The losers, on the other hand, could barely conceal their glee that those cherished positions they had been denied had now lost much of their glitter. For the time being, it was every man for himself; forget the White House (which, for all immediate purposes, was lost anyway) and concentrate on one's own future—get as much personal publicity as possible in the short time remaining no matter what damage to the Candidate might result. McGovern had let them down by the Eagleton fiasco; now they would let him down.

But they still hadn't completely lost hope of eventual victory. The Watergate scandal would catch on as an issue, they said, and when it did, McGovern would have it made. Not one staff member believed for a moment that Nixon, Ehrlichman, Haldeman, Mitchell, Stans, Dean, the CIA, FBI, and The Justice Department were not totally involved in the cover-up. The truth had to come out. Pierre Salinger had once remarked that the campaign was not psychologically prepared for victory. Now it was not psychologically prepared for defeat.

This was, after all, a staff used to the role of underdog.

176 ☐

We had always been behind and had managed to surge ahead in the final days. Even in the primaries we'd lost (which we'd expected to lose), we had closed in at the end, surprising the pollsters, and we had never lost an election we expected to win. We had expected to win this one.

But just in case we didn't, each staff member in his own way was trying to separate himself from the sinking mass, to remind everyone that he was one of the few who had always been against the $1,000-per-person plan and against dropping Eagleton. In fact, now that the polls were registering the full damage of the Eagleton episode, trying to find anyone at headquarters who had advocated dumping him was like trying to turn up a Nazi in post-War Germany.

It was in this cheerful atmosphere that I went to find Frank Mankiewicz, who had made an appointment to talk to me about my new campaign job, now that it didn't appear to be with Jean Westwood. His office was at the end of a corridor on the fourth floor, next to a large cubicle shared by his assistant, Pat Broun, and Gary's assistant, Marcia Johnston.

I would have been well advised to bring along something to read. Failing in such foresight, I started talking to my waiting companions. One was about 33, a top lawyer from another state, whom Frank had promised a big job in the "issues" area of the campaign; the other, a heavy-set man of indeterminate age, who had given up his public relations job after a promise of a job as one of Frank's assistants. Both were glum and, judging from their stiff positions, had spent considerable time in those slat-backed chairs.

Their presence was not an encouraging omen. Trying to keep one eye on Pat's telephone, I glanced

through a three-day-old copy of *The Washington Post.*
From time to time, various staffers carrying stacks of
paper or manila envelopes, conspicuous trademarks of
employment, would pass by giving the three of us dis-
dainful glances. They were In, loved, and belonged,
and we were on display as definitely Out. The sensation
was not unlike sitting outside the school principal's
office during the Parents' Day Picnic.

It was only 2½ hours later, when suddenly Pat Broun
was standing in front of us. She looked at her feet. "Uh,
I'm really sorry," she said, "but Mr. Mankiewicz
wanted me to tell you he had to leave the office suddenly and uh, could you all come back tomorrow?" She
looked acutely pained. "I'm really awfully sorry," she
said again.

The three of us in our row of chairs looked at each
other. The lights on Pat's phone were off, but Frank's
office door was still closed and we were sitting directly
in front of it. The only possible way Frank Mankiewicz
could have left the office without our seeing him was
out the window.

"Quick," said the younger reject, "let's get downstairs. Maybe we can catch him hanging from a sheet!"
They ran off for the back stairs.

It was getting to be a difficult situation to cope with.
Frank Mankiewicz, the Political Director of the Mc-
Govern campaign who had insisted I take this fabulous
job, had turned into Alice in Wonderland's cat—first
you see the cat, then just the eyes, then—poof—nothing at all.

Feeling awkward but not wanting to compound Pat's
obvious embarrassment by looking the way I felt, I hurriedly shuffled off to the ladies room. I emerged five

178 ☐

minutes later and there, down the hall, framed in his doorway was, of all people, Frank Mankiewicz. He spotted me and quickly walking backwards, managed to reenter his office. I, too, stepped out of the hall and into the nearest available space, a janitor's supply closet. It was really perfectly natural. Here I was, the "future Deputy Press Secretary in the White House," cowering in the dark against two wet mops, my foot in a pail, simply waiting for a scheduled appointment with my boss.

Fortunately, it was not as long a wait as I'd had in the chair. Through a crack I watched as Frank again eased himself furtively out of his office—this time carrying a briefcase—and padded on catlike feet down the hall to the elevator. He pushed the down button and the red light lit up the corridor. Ever so casually, I sauntered out of the closet, several strings from the mop still clinging to my hair, and walked over to him.

"Oh, hi there," said Frank with the forced enthusiasm of an airline reservations clerk. "Were you looking for me?"

The elevator arrived and as we rode down, he gave me his latest rendition of "Promises, Promises."

"You're Jean Westwood's Press Secretary," he said matter-of-factly. "I just talked to her this morning and it's all set. And you'll get all your expense money plus all your back salary and a guaranteed salary for the rest of the campaign." Once again, I tried to tell him the actual, somewhat boring facts that I had no job with Jean Westwood, and worse, no money at all.

"It can't be," he said, launching into his regular script, "it just can't be." And then he was the cat again —poof—into a taxi and gone.

☐ *179*

I was certainly now aware that taking a job with the McGovern campaign had been a mistake. But it was the middle of August, the nadir of job openings in New York, I had lent my apartment there to a friend, and I was owed $1,750 in back salary and expenses. If I went back to New York now, I would have no place to live as well as no job and I would feel that I'd been so completely *had* it would probably rankle me the rest of my life. Instead, I decided to be like Tom Eagleton, the dead body which kept turning up in awkward places—in my case, the campaign Treasurer's office. If McGovern lost, I would return immediately to New York and try to pick up my life; if McGovern won, I would also return immediately to New York. But I would get the money I was owed and finish the job I started.

Meanwhile, poor Pierre was back on the chopping block. Having been asked by McGovern to meet with North Vietnamese representatives in Paris to explore the possibility of their releasing some prisoners, Salinger had returned to New York and been greeted by the press. They quoted a UPI story, purportedly leaked by Salinger himself, that at McGovern's instruction, he had told the North Vietnamese that McGovern wanted the War ended as soon as possible, despite the effect it might have on his own election chances. Not having succeeded with a prisoner release deal, Pierre had apparently leaked a story which would make McGovern look good and, at the same time, put Salinger, who had been made to look ridiculous by McGovern and the press, back on the political map. Before commenting to reporters, Pierre called McGovern, campaigning in Springfield, Illinois. He missed him by four minutes. Meanwhile, questioned about the UPI story, McGovern, not having talked to Pierre and furious about another leak, made a sweeping denial, implying that not only was the story itself untrue but also the fact that he had ever sent Pierre to Paris. Later, after talking to Pierre, he modified his response, denying the UPI story but asserting that, yes, he *had*, as a matter of fact, sent Pierre to Paris. It was strange that he had forgotten because he had originally suggested sending Pierre to Hanoi.

Back at headquarters, we all gathered to watch the evening news, the "daily bummer," as it was called, on Henry Kimelman's color television set, and there they were, McGovern's denial and his nondenial cleanly spliced to run back to back in the show. Our credibility gap had widened.

Pierre returned to Washington and was named a Co-chairman of Citizens for McGovern, an umbrella organization for citizens' groups which, according to the plan, would spring up all over the country, and could, if successful enough, win us the election. Finally, I was given the dubious job of Press Director of Citizens, working with former McCarthy leader Reverend Joe Duffey and a small, young, and charmingly nonpolitical staff.

In an office on the fifth floor of the Watergate, we put together and publicized the formation of independent organizations for McGovern: Physicians, Faculty Members, Lawyers, Businessmen, Athletes, Aerospace Workers, Americans Abroad, Scientists, Religious Leaders, and others, all out there working hard for McGovern and hopefully, convincing their colleagues to do the same.

I liked working at the Watergate. There was a Howard Johnson's just across the street which sold mocha chip and Jamoca almond fudge ice cream and a Danish pastry shop on the Watergate's lower level. Aside from our weekly bomb scares, the office resembled real life. We were unified in trying to do one job in the campaign and we talked to each other and laughed. With the exception of me, everyone else was new on the job, so there was none of the bitterness of the K Street office and for the first time in my campaign experience, no intrigue.

Unfortunately for me, however, there was also no money. Despite Frank's promises, I'd seen no salary since July 15 and the campaign now owed me $2,250 in back promises. Gary and Frank were getting paychecks as were their assistants, as were Henry Kimelman, Marian Pearlman, and I suspected, quite a few others. Not only that, but each day I read at least one newspaper article quoting fund raiser Morris Dees with his latest excited accounts of mounting accumulations of cash in the McGovern coffers. Certainly a tiny portion of it could go to a devoted employee. So once again, I set out for the K Street headquarters.

Frank could not, of course, be disturbed that day and he was about to go out of town, but Pat Broun remembered seeing a "reinstatement of salary" form for me which she was certain had been sent to Marian Pearlman. Apparently, the Campaign Managers had taken almost everyone off salary at different points in the campaign in somewhat the same way that *Life* magazine thinned out its subscription list just before dropping it entirely. Afterward, many of those initially dropped McGovern workers had conveniently faded away, leaving fewer of them to contend with now.

Up on the seventh floor, in an effortless gesture toward Women's Lib, a clever little sign pointed the way to the offices of "Marian Pearlperson" and "Henry Kimelperson." Henry Kimelperson was out to lunch and Marian Pearlperson was able to muster as much concern over the financial needs of Kristi Poorperson as a landlord over the business setbacks of his tenant.

"I never received a notice for you," she said with her customary long-distance telephone operator warmth. "You have to see George Cunningham down on the first floor. He's the only one who can approve any salary."

I didn't want to see George Cunningham. He was a small, forgettable-looking man, slightly balding, with a round face and glasses who didn't look frightening but who scared me. He had a single-minded approach to almost every problem and I believed he would single-mindedly see that I never saw a paycheck.

He didn't disappoint me. "Frank Mankiewicz," he squeaked, straining over his desk from his position atop two telephone books, "has no authority whatsoever over salaries. I have never seen any notice about you from him but even if I did have one, it would be valueless. The only person who can approve salaries is Gary Hart."

So back I went up four floors to see Gary Hart. "He has someone with him," said Marcia, "but you can wait." I was back in the same chair where I had waited in vain for Frank Mankiewicz two weeks before and I hoped before the afternoon was over I wouldn't be back in the broom closet as well.

But this time, I was luckier. After only a little over an hour, Marcia came over to me. "Gary knows why you're here," she said, "but he'll have to clear any payment with Frank and now Frank's just gone out of town. Why don't you go see Marian Pearlman?"

Dejectedly, I trailed back to the Watergate to write some more cheery press releases about all the McGovern organizations springing up around the country, the money pouring in, and the swarms of people desperately eager to hold fund raisers.

One of the first citizens-type fund raisers was a picnic and concert at Ethel Kennedy's house at the end of August. Apparently, the opportunity to see the home of the Kennedys and hear a little music was sufficient enticement for some 6,000 people to jam all routes to McLean, Virginia, during the evening rush hour in order to unburden themselves of $15 for the McGovern cause.

It was a hot, sultry afternoon when the first hordes arrived on the huge green lawn, carrying assorted children and blankets. Sadly for them, they were not carrying picnic suppers, an omission which could not be blamed on them since the widely advertised $15 event clearly included a picnic supper. And, indeed, at the end of the driveway was a long food table, attended by several young boys, behind a labyrinthian fence-like apparatus to separate the lines of people.

The problem was that even after they had waited for some forty minutes, what the people were offered to eat was barely distinguishable from the table itself—a cold, paper-thin McDonald burger, having spent so long in its stale unbuttered bun as to have adhered to it for life, a bag of potato chips, and a sticky orange drink. Not exactly what you'd expect at the Kennedys'.

But then, hardly any Kennedys were there—no Ethel, no Teddy or Joan, no Sarge or Eunice Shriver, no George or Eleanor McGovern—only a smattering of McGovern and Kennedy children: 22-year-old Kathleen, barefoot and in her brother's baggy corduroy

184 ☐

pants, and 19-year-old Joe in his own baggy pants.

It was oppressively hot on the lawn but you couldn't go into the house; nor could you go near other areas such as the pool, pool house, tennis court, or most sections of grass. Should you forget and approach any of these places, you were reminded by ropes and signs that they were definitely "off limits." On limits was the center of the lawn near an erected concert stage, the "food" table, and if you could find them, the portable johns.

None of this would have been upsetting—it was, after all, the Kennedys' home to do with as they liked—if only the rules had applied to all the people. But they didn't. Conspicuously cordoned off by ropes and guarded by McGovern staffers was a large area, including the pool, its flagstone terrace, and comfortable pool house. Ostensibly, it was reserved for the use of the concert entertainers; but with them, sitting on comfortable deck chairs, sipping gin and tonics, and devouring plates of lamb, salad, and cake in full view of the assembled hungry crowd of 6,000 paying guests, was a large group of special McGovern staff members, special reporters who were friends of the staff, and special fat cats. I couldn't help feeling that once again the McGovern staff, by setting up such a visibly elitist arrangement, was presenting the worst possible image of our widely promoted People's Campaign.

Meanwhile, out on the road, McGovern was being overadvised. He should be more active, said Hubert Humphrey; he should be more serious, said Stewart Udall; and Frank Mankiewicz talked him into a flying media campaign. "They're only going to show one event a day on TV in Los Angeles," said Frank, "so why should we do two?" when instead, the Candidate could be whisked back and forth across the country via his new chartered jet, hitting three different media markets and three different news shows a day.

Again, it was a strange reaction for the major spokesman for the People's Campaign. Dashing from state to state in a panicky search for television cameras hardly seemed the way for McGovern to learn the problems of a state or meet more than a handful of its residents. But the schedulers ordained it, and, obviously not having learned anything from the mistakes of John Lindsay, for the moment media impact was their god.

Even though we were, as McGovern admitted, "lagging" in the polls (somewhere in the neighborhood of 23% to 63%), the traveling advisors still expected a gradual climb until we sprinted ahead with our customary last-minute dash at the November 7 finish line. "There is no doubt in our minds, on the eve of the formal kickoff of this campaign," said Gary, "that the McGovern-Shriver ticket will win."

Meanwhile, Gordon Weil, having been dropped from the traveling entourage, was busy in the Washington office writing and proofreading position papers. Having discovered his $1,000-income-grant proposal a rankling thorn in big business's side, Weil killed off the income grant for good and, with a group of prominent economists and businessmen, helped put together a new package of tax and welfare reform proposals, which McGovern had explained in his Wall Street speech of August 29. "Remember," said Weil, "these are just suggestions to be considered by Congress, nothing to be locked into." Afterward, most Wall Streeters, though not exactly ecstatic, had at least toned down some of their criticisms. Most important, the speech had been generally commended as thorough and well documented. Weil was rewarded for his effort by being named Executive Director of the campaign. He had, after all, been in from the start.

Out on the road, McGovern had found a theme for his campaign—the struggle between light and darkness. He talked about truth and goodness and decency, his virtues which he seemed to believe should be credentials enough to carry him straight to the White House. He raged about the ITT scandal, the grain scandal, the milk scandal, the Watergate scandal, Nixon's secret campaign funds, Nixon's secret plan to raise taxes and continue the War, all part of a seething bed of Republican corruption. He sounded right, and righteous. "I'd vote for George McGovern for God," someone said.

But with all his Biblical phrases, George McGovern forgot some of the most important history in the Bible —that you can be Right and Good but it doesn't always work out.

While McGovern struggled across the country in an endless sea of faces, his staff back in Washington was doing everything possible to rock the boat. First, Larry O'Brien threatened to quit as Campaign Chairman unless some clear lines of authority were set up to replace the current division of leadership among himself, Mankiewicz, Hart, and Westwood in Washington and Fred Dutton on the road. No one knows where the buck stops, he said. He was right, of course, but this problem should have been solved long before in a quiet meeting, not brought to the attention, as it now was, of the entire readership of *The New York Times*. As usual, nameless middle-level officials felt called upon to add their damaging few words to *The Times* article. "We're living in unmitigated chaos," said one, "People are spending half their time plotting against other people in the campaign." True, but also not too helpful to George McGovern when viewed in *The Times.*

Another "well-placed source" revealed more staff dissentions: Jean Westwood's efforts to strip Gary Hart of his field operation responsibilities; problems in California where Jewish residents resented Western States Coordinator Rick Stearns, who as a student leader had once signed an anti-Zionist tract; problems in Connecticut; problems in New York where Joe Grandmaison had quit over Gary Hart's attempts to put that campaign into the hands of an experienced politician, Howard Samuels (Grandmaison had later returned); strife everywhere between inexperienced state coordinators and regular party leaders; and the embarrassment over "Shriverisms," Shriver's proclivity for taking positions, by mistake, in direct contradiction to McGovern's.

Who were these "middle-level officials" and "well-placed sources"? Obviously disgruntled staffers. The fire had finally raged out of control. No longer were they content to burn each other; now they had to destroy the whole forest—to kill off the Campaign completely.

Then, just when even the conservative *Wall Street Journal* noted that McGovern's "trouble-ridden presidential campaign finally is on the upswing," the staff hit him again. After a fight with Mrs. Westwood and Gary Hart over campaign control in New Jersey, Representative Frank Thompson quit as head of that state's National Voter Registration drive. Even mild-mannered Ted Van Dyk, Director of Research, walked out, remarking that "the staff infighting was like fighting for staterooms on the Titanic." But no one believed he was gone for good. It was a Friday and he hadn't taken his Rollodex. (They were right. He returned Monday.) And that afternoon, Gordon Weil announced that he, too, had quit.

What caused the Weil outburst was a conflict with Gary Hart over a mailing printed without a union bug. The mailing would have to be redone, said Weil. No way, said Hart. Both turned to McGovern, who backed Hart 1,000%. Gary fired Gordon, and Gordon stormed out, but not before he had scooped up his Rollodex, the latter gesture indicating a departure of some permanence. Not so. The next day, Weil returned with a "reports that I am leaving are erroneous" statement to the press, and life resumed as usual.

Campaigning in Texas, McGovern felt understandably betrayed. "Here I am out here belting away and these things happen," he said. "I feel as though I'm up in outer space headed for the moon and the guys down at NASA are walking off the job."

Asked who might quit next, Press Secretary Dick Dougherty quipped, "If this keeps up maybe it will be George McGovern!"

Finally, having purged themselves in print, some of the staff quieted down. Whole days passed without a single middle-level conspirator leaking news to the press. But then the jealousy started again.

Ted Kennedy had joined McGovern's traveling campaign for several days turning it into the crowd-packing George and Teddy Show. Ten thousand people gathered to cheer them in Albany, other thousands in Pittsburgh, Boston, and Waterbury, Connecticut. They came to see Kennedy but they heard McGovern, and when he talked about the thing he felt most deeply, the immorality of the Vietnam War, the fervor of applause

☐ *189*

surprised even Kennedy, who now both publicly and privately predicted that the polls would really turn around.

With poor crowds and bad press for the traveling campaign, those Washington staffers left behind had had little to envy. Now, with Teddy along and the general mood improving, they began to suspect that the traveling campaign was having fun, that those along on it were in the center of the action, meeting important people and being noticed themselves. Jealousy at headquarters raged once again.

No one seemed to remember that this was a Presidential campaign, not a carnival—that there was work to be done and, usually, the best place to do it is on the ground. No matter, The Plane was Nirvana, and the campaign was destined to suffer a dirth of talent on earth with an overwhelming top heaviness in the air.

I began to wonder if the Watergate scandal went even further than McGovern and the newspapers were now suggesting. Perhaps Nixon's operatives had accomplished the ultimate—they had staffed McGovern's campaign!

chapter 10

Have You Seen
a Bugger About?

As September moved into October, life in Washington became more bearable physically. The sodden humidity and relentlessly beating sun slowly gave way to clearer skies and a faint hint of crispness in the early morning air.

And though not at all hopeful about my own future, I was becoming more so about McGovern's. At last, the Watergate scandal seemed to be catching on. Everything we had been saying about it was proving to be true. Kenneth Clawson, former White House Deputy Director of Communications, was reputed to have bragged to a reporter that he had been the author of the Muskie "Canuck" letter. Afterward he denied it, but later it came out that another Nixonian, former White House Special Counsel Charles Colson, had written the newspaper ad purportedly by the group of "citizens" supporting Nixon's mining of Haiphong Harbor. A spy, Donald Segretti it was discovered, had been hired by CREEP (Committee to Re-elect the President) to sabotage the campaigns of the Democratic candidates; phones had been bugged; files and schedules had been stolen, campaign appearances disrupted, all part of a wide sinister network of Republican Gestapo operations. News was also coming out that in both Nixon's

☐ *193*

'60 and '68 campaigns for President and his 1962 campaign for Governor of California, Haldeman had been involved in unethical campaign practices, which included the mailing of a phony pro-Nixon poll in 1962 supposedly sponsored by "The Committee for the Preservation of the Democratic Party" (CPDP)—which could have been translated "The Committee to Put Dick in Power." That tactic had failed, but it now seemed a logical conclusion that most of the public relations reports emanating from the White House might have the Haldeman touch.

In fact, that touch went way back, even to Haldeman's college days, where at UCLA he and his later White House comrade, John Ehrlichman, were classmates. At that time, Haldeman had run the campaign of Ehrlichman's wife for Class President, and had employed some of the same questionable tactics.

For many McGovern campaign workers, the sabotage news was a delicious umbrella under which to hide a few goof-ups. Suddenly, *all* the mistakes were sabotage, things most of us hadn't heard of until now, such as Gary Hart's reported phone call to George Meany just before the New York primary, during which he had very arrogantly insisted Meany come to New York to meet with McGovern. It wasn't me, said Gary in September. It was, said Meany. How could you know the truth? There was so much arrogance and rudeness in the campaign anything was possible, but Gary was not in New York the day the call was supposedly made. There were some incidents, however, which could only be sabotage; scheduled campaign appearances by McGovern suddenly canceled by a phone call, a call to CBS from a McGovern media buyer canceling a major commercial, a call to Walter Cronkite supposedly from

194 ☐

Frank Mankiewicz thanking him for being so consistently pro-McGovern. But were the Republicans doing it or McGovern's own angry and jealous staff? If it was the Republicans, they needn't have bothered. The Democrats were their own worst enemies.

Then one day, our suspicions were justified. Nestled comfortably deep within Spencer Oliver's telephone upstairs at the DNC, was a bug. The police arrived, reporters and photographers swarmed through the building, and all of us were questioned. Naturally, there was great speculation over why it was Spencer Oliver's phone. His job didn't involve secrets and shouldn't have made him a particularly interesting catch. More jealousy in headquarters. With the bug discovery, Oliver's name was mentioned repeatedly in the papers, he was interviewed on television, his bug was photographed. Now everybody wanted one. It was, after all, rather a status symbol; you wouldn't rate a bug if you weren't pretty big (later it turned out that he was bugged by mistake; the Waterbuggers thought they had Larry O'Brien's phone). I must also admit a certain disappointment when my phone was dismantled and found clean. But while the phone sweeps were going on, the staff was not idle. The rumor went out that Spencer Oliver had bugged himself in order to get attention and look important. Now I fully expected an assortment of homemade versions to pop up in various middle-level phones, but the electronic sophistication in the campaign was, perhaps, not up to the job. Oliver maintained his image as the DNC's only bugee.

Back on August 28, Attorney General Richard Kleindienst had pledged that the Justice Department investigation would be "the most extensive, thorough and comprehensive investigation since the assassination of

President Kennedy." And he lived up to his word. Now each day we could look forward to interrogation by a fleet of earnest-faced, short-haired agents, cruising about with clipboards, hard at work gathering statistics for their exhaustive survey. It had to be a diversionary tactic because they even interviewed me.

"What have you seen?" Nothing. "Where have you been?" Nowhere. "What do you do?" Get coffee . . . Xerox . . . pray for money. "Have you noticed anything unusual about your telephone?" Only that no one interesting ever calls me. "Do you know Spencer Oliver?" No. "Do you know why they'd bug his phone?" Haven't the remotest. "Have you observed anything strange?" The whole campaign. "Have you seen any buggers about?" What??? Where????

And so it went. "Asking Richard Kleindienst to investigate the Watergate," said Frank Mankiewicz, "is like asking Al Capone to investigate the Mafia." He was right.

Out on the road, McGovern still tried to bring the Watergate scandal to the attention of the sleeping electorate. "The Nixon Administration is the most corrupt in two centuries of American government," he said in Seattle, "one of wiretappers, warmongers, and purveyors of racial fear. Political manipulation started in California," he reminded the residents of that Golden State. "It started with Murray Chotiner and Richard Nixon— that same tricky pair that is operating again in 1972 . . . a White House filled with clever public relations experts whose function is to manipulate public opinion."

"History shows us," he told a press conference in New Mexico, "it is but a single step from spying on the political opposition to suppressing that opposition and

196 □

the imposing of a one-party state in which the people's precious liberties are lost. Government officials who will condone the Watergate episode would have no qualms tomorrow about violating the privacy of the voting booth, or the church, or your home if it were necessary to carry out their purposes."

Later, the most respected Senators and Congressmen from both parties would say exactly the same thing, and the public would care and talk of little else; but right now, America wasn't listening to George McGovern.

McGovern was still trying to run a 1960's campaign. But the '60's had ended in 1968 with the election of Richard Nixon. We were really back in the '50's. It was already a depressing year on top of a succession of depressing years: rising prices, falling stock market, scandals, the War, crime. Who wanted to think about goodness and justice and truth just now? It only reminded you of how little of it was around. Not many people trusted Nixon, but he wasn't taking away their money, or so they believed. No one knew whether to trust McGovern, but he was threatening to take away their money, so why bother to find out? Why listen?

And so, McGovern tried to reach them with the biggest issue of all, the one which had started him on his rocky, futile quest for the Presidency, the War in Vietnam. He would give a major speech about it on October 10, the first of four fireside chats on the issues.

What happened with the Vietnam speech pointed up some of the larger problems in the campaign. Former Secretary of Defense Clark Clifford raced against the clock to get the first draft of the speech ready. But McGovern didn't like it. Ted Van Dyk tried a draft. But word came back from McGovern's top Vietnam advisor, John Holum, that the Candidate didn't like it, either, but would use parts and fill in the rest. Van Dyk waited nervously to see the next draft. It didn't appear. So the night before the taping of the speech, Van Dyk and Mankiewicz met McGovern at the airport as he returned from a campaign swing and demanded to see his changes. No, they said, after reading the McGovern version, much too much Scripture—lines like "forgive them Father for they know not what they do" just won't make it with the electorate. No one wants to hear how bad he is even if it's true; that stuff has to go. O. K., said McGovern, I'll go home and work on it. "We'll *all* work on it together," said Van Dyk and Mankiewicz. A compromise was worked out. McGovern would work on it alone, but all three would meet the next morning to go over the final version. They met and McGovern read the speech aloud. There were still about twelve Scriptural passages. No, said Mankiewicz and Van Dyk again. No. No. No. So once more McGovern dutifully scratched out the Scriptures and went off to his taping alone. Once rid of Mankiewicz and Van Dyk, however, he eased some of them back in. What, after all, was a good speech without Scripture? He hadn't had to accept their ideas, he hadn't been forced into a corner, and most importantly, he'd stayed flexible. Mankiewicz and Van Dyk were the ones who ended up not knowing what was going on. He did.

Even with the Scriptures, it was a very moving speech. "Mr. Nixon has described the Vietnam war as our finest hour," said McGovern. "I regard it as the saddest chapter in our national history. Our sons have asked for jobs—and we've sent them to an Asian jungle. Our sons have asked for an education—and we've taught them how to kill. Our sons have asked for a full measure of time—and 50,000 of them have been lost before their time . . . So, let us seize the chance to lift from our sons and ourselves the terror of this war, and bestow the blessings of peace. And then we can restore our sense of purpose and our character as a great nation . . . Let us head the ancient words: 'I have set before you life and death, blessing and cursing. Therefore, choose life, that thou and thy seed may live.' "

From my vantage point in Washington, the speech changed the mood of the campaign. A week later, Morris Dees announced an influx of $577,220.87 to our treasury, and Miles Rubin waxed enthusiastically about how we were "constantly meeting our cash flow problem" and paying all our bills.

Just not mine, apparently. I was now a prime potential recipient for one of McGovern's $1,000 income grants, or three of them, actually, since I was now owed $3,200 by the campaign. Despite continued promises from Frank and Pierre, I was losing hope that any of it would ever come my way.

But other good things were happening. A weekly campaign newsletter began to circulate encouraging news; our voter registration drive would break all records, with Democrats outnumbering Republicans 5,-599,087 to 3,670,244 in California, 1.2 million to 483,-623 in Maryland. There appeared to be a drop in Nixon's lead in certain key states, a growing disparity between our poll by Pat Caddell and those by Gallup and Yankelovich, and a growing belief that George McGovern might just be right when he called those other polls "rubbish . . . things made up in the back room somewhere."

Even Shriver had pulled his act together and, aside

from an uncanny ability to always get himself photographed at the precise moment that he dropped pizza on his chin, he was otherwise an exuberant, articulate candidate.

With the mood of the campaign looking up, you would have thought everyone on the staff might have been working hard. Wrong. The mailroom closed at 5:00 p.m., the Xerox and mimeograph rooms were locked by 5:30, hardly anyone worked on weekends, and, even on weekdays, the earliest you could detect a human presence was generally around 9:30 a.m. Pierre, when he was around, was a voice in the wilderness. "In the Kennedy campaign, people worked around the clock," he would say to anyone who would listen—but hardly anyone would. "The mailroom never closed, weekends were like week days . . ." Neither he nor Frank had ever fully accepted the fact that in no way was this another Kennedy campaign.

One mistake all along, of course, was that McGovern misread the desirability of youth. More young were in power in this campaign than in any before it, a point his top advisors constantly emphasized to enforce our image of the "new politics."

Because he started out as such a dark horse and off to the left side of political thinking, McGovern naturally attracted the young, whom he could offer campaign jobs with fancy titles, not normally accessible to such inexperienced people. His campaign was at first a minor effort appropriately run by minors, but as he came up, they felt they owned him and were determined not to share him. The candidate became their captive and they, in time, his limitation. These kids had always had wildly impractical, rigid, theological notions about poli-

200 ☐

tics, but because McGovern failed to take complete control, they went wild, like "an unruly classroom," wrote columnist Tom Braden.

To me, the campaign was rather like a Christmas tree with the top chopped off. Without a point and a star, the middle (where the balls were, so to speak) became the focal point. There, everyone had a title which suggested he was the boss. In fact, no one was.

To most of the kids the goal of winning the nomination meant beating out the Regulars and vindicating McCarthy's defeat and Kennedy's death in 1968. But once the nomination was won, they weren't up to the campaign itself. And youthful energy and enthusiasm, it turned out, didn't make up for a lack of common sense and knowledge. Like a driver's education class, these kids could do perfectly well sitting in their chairs in class, or driving on quiet country roads or on the highway with the instructor, but God forbid when they were out on that highway alone and suddenly forced to make a snap judgment in a situation never faced before.

Often they had never heard of the politicians they snubbed, and didn't recognize the names of the professionally experienced Democrats offering help. In selecting Eagleton, no one ever thought of asking an opinion of the Governor of his state, Warren Hearnes, who apparently knew and would have revealed Eagleton's medical history. Like children, it was easier to defy the grownups and pit themselves against those "evil old pros" than try for compromise.

And again, it was amateurism which on nomination night made them turn away Governor Hearnes of Missouri whom Eagleton had asked to second his nomination. No, said the McGovernites. He was "old politics."

Instead they would only accept a black, a Chicano, and a woman. Hearnes was rudely disinvited.

Like children in the clubhouse, they rejoiced in the public humiliation of those kept out—Mayor Daley of Chicago, labor leaders, even Larry O'Brien, who represented a bridge between the old and the new.

McGovern's preoccupation with the youth cult led him to accept unquestioningly Fred Dutton's opinion that the new 18 year old vote would control this election and that we could win simply by registering millions of new voters. His reliance on youth may also have been responsible for his misreading the mood of the country. He so jealously guarded his position on the left that he never noticed no one else was there—except his staff.

At a dinner at McGovern's house in August, Washington columnist Roger Wilkins told McGovern bluntly that his staff was killing him, that he'd be finished unless he took firm control. But McGovern's reaction indicated the depth of the problem. He wasn't willing to change his action; he justified it. He wanted someone else to cope. "I've tried, I've threatened to fire them but I just can't control them," he was quoted as saying. He was unlucky, he complained. Jack Kennedy had Bobby to take care of his staff, Bobby had Steve Smith, but he, George, had no one, no brother or relative. And it was unfair, he went on, to criticize his handling of the Eagleton affair. Eisenhower, after all, hadn't been able to get rid of his poor choice for Vice President, Richard Nixon, and Nixon hadn't been able to get rid of Agnew. If they couldn't do it at *all*, why should he be blamed for not doing it *well?*

He was pointing up what Pat Caddell was discovering in the polls—that people thought McGovern was a nice guy but one who couldn't achieve. He might be right, but no one believed there was any muscle behind the virtue. They didn't take him seriously.

"A lot of us have just given up," said Ed O'Donnell. "Very early this campaign turned into a battle between the forces of decency and antidecency. If you tried to act, to get something done efficiently, you came up against the jealousy of the anti-decency forces, and they were always in charge and always won. The only way to survive was never to deal with them, which really meant never to do anything. Gary Hart figured that out early. He managed to keep his position but not making any decisions. Most of us, though, ended up with two choices—to quit or to stay on and do nothing. And we reasoned, why be masochistic and quit? Let the campaign quit."

My own job had now deteriorated to the point of nonexistence. Once we'd organized all the citizens groups I no longer needed to write press releases about them. I now spent most of my day at the Xerox machine, on the telephone straightening out minor conflicts in Pierre Salinger's lecture schedule, or enroute here or there for coffee and ice cream. And once in a while, between trips, when Pierre made one of his rare appearances at the office, he gave me the privilege of taking his laundry to the laundromat.

"I've made a decision," I announced one day, staggering in with an exceptionally large laundry load, "I'm going to write a book."

"What sort of book?" asked Pierre, diverting his attention for the first time from a shirt count to me.

"Oh, I don't know, maybe about what it's like to be a girl working in a campaign like this. At least, that way I might make some MONEY."

"That's the worst idea I've ever heard," said Pierre slowly, now ignoring his laundry completely and lighting a particularly pungent cigar. "How could you even *think* of doing a thing like that? Do you want to be the Mary Gallagher of the McGovern campaign? It's a terrible, terrible idea."

"No," I said dejectedly, "of course not." I couldn't let Pierre down. After all, he had been one of the loyalest people around.

Now, without even the slight hope of recouping some of my loss with a book, I began waking up at 4 a.m. every morning thinking about my life. That thought, of course, threw me into a state of instant total panic as visions of my lost television job loomed about my bed, which, at that hour, always seemed to be floating above a bottomless pit. Maybe I wasn't going to get through it after all; maybe this once-in-a-lifetime experience would result in the end of a lifetime. I needed help.

Fortunately, it was nearby. One of the citizens' groups I had helped organize, Physicians for McGovern, had had an important offshoot—Psychiatrists for McGovern. Now I needed the whole organization.

I settled for just one, however, a doctor who kindly answered my frantic 6 a.m. phone call and who, having himself invested a great deal of time and money in the campaign, understood my problem. He even agreed to see me several times for free.

Besides suffering from acute insomnia, manic depression, and engulfing despair, I was also, in the last weeks of the campaign, consumed by another unusual behavioral trait, usually only associated with prison inmates.

204 □

This was an overwhelming preoccupation with time— the time left until the end of the campaign. I had noticed this symptom one day in early August when I had been faced with the unhappy realization that I still had 92 days to go until it was over. Repeatedly, I had tried to analyze how 92 days *felt* in a desperate attempt to make the period seem shorter. I remembered how fast the summers went by when I was a child, but that didn't help enough; they weren't 92 days long, more in the neighborhood of 74 days. But I'd tell myself how short a time 18 days could seem if you were having fun —that's just 2 weeks and 4 days, add 18 and 74 and you take care of the whole 92. As we moved downward into each new group of figures—the 80's, 70's, 60's, and 50's, I felt increasingly better, but I couldn't break the habit. I still recounted several times a day just to be sure.

In my life, time had always gone the fastest when I traveled, and, luckily, I now got that chance. I could go back on the traveling campaign for the last 2 weeks. Actually, I couldn't afford not to. The last photographs I had taken for *Time* had been several weeks before— of Ethel Kennedy at a picnic at the Shrivers about to pour a glass of beer over musician Neil Diamond's head. Now to live up to the rest of my photo contract, I had to take some pictures of McGovern.

On October 25, I flew to Detroit with Frank Mankiewicz, (who was in high spirits over the latest developments in the Watergate scandal) to join the traveling road show which would take us to Iowa, California, and Washington State.

It was fun to rejoin old reporter friends and once again be part of what seemed like a normal group of people. That first evening McGovern gave a speech to a large group of women at Detroit's Hazel Park High

School. He looked rested, seemed confident, and was wildly cheered. When he finished his speech, he stepped off the stage, and, flanked by Dougherty and Weil, began working his way through the crowd toward an exit where several of us were standing. McGovern saw me and suddenly stopped, gave a big smile, and reached his hand over the heads of a group of autograph seekers.

"Hi, Kristi," he said. "We've missed you for the last few weeks. Hope you'll stay around for a while now." That was what I liked best about George McGovern—on a one-to-one basis, he was a kind, thoughtful, ordinary man, a bit indecisive like the rest of us but someone whom I didn't think could possibly be aware of all the behind-the-scenes machinations of his staff.

The next morning as we gathered in front of the Howard Johnson Motel to board buses for the airport, word came that Henry Kissinger was about to hold a televised press conference. The one television set in Howard Johnson's was turned on and we heard him announce that "peace is at hand."

The lack of response was interesting. Assorted hotel guests, groping for their morning Danish and coffee, seemed mildly disturbed by the onslaught of 100 newsmen into the bar but otherwise disinterested in the Kissinger statement. Reporters scribbled down the facts but even the McGovern staff seemed unperturbed. "The Republicans will look so phony announcing this two weeks before the election that the whole thing may backfire and lose them votes . . ." seemed to be the general reaction.

At the airport, I was amazed by the luxuries the campaign had acquired since the early days. There, on the runway, side by side, sat three United Airlines jets, their massive wings glistening in the sun. The Senator's plane, the *Dakota Queen II*, named after McGovern's World War II B-24 bomber, carried McGovern, Mankiewicz, Dougherty, Dutton, and whatever dignitaries happened to be along, as well as 32 seats' worth of the traveling press corps. The second one, the traditional campaign "Zoo" plane, carried television cameramen, technicians, still photographers with their heavy equipment, and some other reporters. The third carried anything left over. I picked the third one, a standard three-row-seat style jet, for the first lap of the trip to Iowa, after which I had been assigned to the *Dakota Queen* for the cross-country flight to California. I was thrilled to discover that the third plane had some 60 empty seats; maybe the days of bumping were over.

If the rally at Iowa State University was any indication of George McGovern's appeal outside Washington, D.C., it seemed to me that we had the election won. The cheering crowd of between 8,000 and 10,000 people completely filled an enormous mall between two university buildings, and spilled out beyond it farther than you could see. Students, faculty, and onlookers were everywhere—on every nearby rooftop, on window ledges, balconies, and even in trees. Here they were, an antiwar crowd, cheering McGovern and booing Nixon, whose emissary Henry Kissinger had, just three hours before, announced peace.

"I've always thought a settlement of the war before the election would help me," McGovern later said. "It would tend to show people that I was right all along about the possibility of ending the war . . . When I said I'd get us out of the war within 90 days of becoming

President, everyone including Richard Nixon said it couldn't be done. Now here's Nixon saying he can do it in 60 days."

It was hard, standing there at Iowa State University, to be unaffected by the crowd's surging enthusiasm and hope and not to wonder if perhaps George McGovern, daily mobbed by crowds like these, knew more about the mood of the American people than did Richard Nixon in the White House or George Gallup in Princeton.

"Help us be all we can be," said an enormous sign held up by the students.

On the *Dakota Queen*, buoyed by the enormous earthbound crowds, a mood of success permeated our feelings and thoughts. Up close, George McGovern did not look or act like a loser, as I had expected he now might. He behaved like the next President of the United States. Even so, I noticed that neither he nor his running mate were treated with a preponderance of respect. Shriver, on his campaign plane was referred to by press and staff as "the yoyo," while McGovern remained affectionately "McGoo."

Jules Witcover and Walter Mears (an AP reporter) wrote a song about it to the tune of "What Do You Do When You Fall in Love":

> What do you do when you're George McGoo?
> Pick a veep and then you dump him,
> Read the polls and see you're slumpin',
> I wish I had a chance to win. . . .

And they had another one, too, based on the repeated campaign stops in Ohio.

> Why oh why oh why oh
> Do we keep going to Ohio. . . .

208 □

"We sang it to him one day," said Jules, "and boy, were we sorry. He gave us a long tedious explanation of all the reasons Ohio was important for the election!"

But though he was kidded, George McGovern remained good-natured and available. When I walked into the front cabin of the plane, he was leaning back in an armchair with his hands in back of his head, while Frank Mankiewicz sat across from him reading over speech notes, his feet propped up on the table between them.

I photographed them both and as I did, they autographed some other pictures I'd taken a month before. I was briefly encouraged by Frank's inscription: "For Kristi—Love and some day, money—Frank."

"I think," said McGovern, signing one of himself in an exceptionally friendly crowd, "that it's really turning around. [The switch was on?] Texas is coming around, and Michigan, and a lot of people are now coming back to us. I truly believe I'm going to win; I really have faith in the American people's integrity and common sense."

In the evening, we landed in Sacramento where I scrambled to the air freight office to ship my film to New York—heart pounding with fear that I would somehow be left behind—and then to another rally, this time indoors, but with the same packed and frenzied crowds shouting "Four more months" (time left for Nixon) and "We want George."

We danced from Sacramento to Los Angeles in the back compartment of the plane, drinks spilling on the mimeograph machines and music blaring from a loudspeaker, singing another Witcover-Mears song, this one an adaptation from a well-known Broadway musical—

☐ *209*

"Mankiewicz—Superstar—Put out the light in Pierre's cigar. . . ."

Ted Kennedy joined us the next day for an emotional rally at North Hollywood's Laurel Plaza Shopping Center. Again, watching the intent looks on faces in the crowd and hearing the cheers, I sensed as I had on a similar day in 1968 when I had come to Los Angeles with the losing Humphrey campaign, an enormous build up of momentum. That time, just 2 days before the election, I had felt the same surge of excitement and had believed that the mood was turning around. It almost had. "If there had only been one more week." they had all said afterwards. This time we had that one more week.

chapter 11

Sorry, You Need a Reservation for the Life Boat

Our next campaign stop was Spokane, Washington, for a rally at Gonzaga University and another cheering crowd of about 6,000. A wild array of signs bobbed up and down, one of which had been showing up more and more lately, "I'd rather pick a green apple than a rotten one." Maybe McGovern's moral theme was finally catching on.

"This election is the choice of a century," he told the crowd. "How long will our liberty last if our highest officials wiretap at will, burglarize the opposition, intimidate the press, and engage in forgery, sabotage, and spying?

"How long will our freedom endure if our people must endure a tax system that is not fair? We are not free in the real sense if our government is put on the auction block to special interests and the truth is put into a paper shredder."

In these last weeks, besides trying to reach voters with the choice between good and evil, he was also trying to reach them through question and answer telethons. We had done a number of them already and one more awaited us at Spokane's KING-TV.

It was a nice idea but there were two big problems with telethons. One, they never worked electronically;

☐ *213*

and two, the average person who phoned in appeared to have the intelligence level of a German shepherd dog with a reading problem.

At each telethon, McGovern would sit in a studio armchair, wearing a blue suit and shirt against a blue backdrop, and facing a studio audience arranged on banks of seats. A telephone next to him would ring, he would answer and a loudspeaker would broadcast the viewer's question and McGovern's answer to the TV and studio audiences.

Spokane's KING-TV lived up to its predecessors. McGovern picked up the receiver. "Hello," he said, smiling at the telephone. "This is George McGovern. Can you hear me? I'm ready for your question." Dead silence. "Hello?" "Hello?" Embarrassment and a strong sense of déjà vu setting in for McGovern, staff, and press who have been through it all before.

"Uh, we seem to be having a little—uh—technical problem," McGovern says, still smiling. Now a chance for a good line developed during similar past episodes. "If you'll just be patient, they'll have the problem corrected in no time. We Democrats just don't seem to be as good with these electronic devices as the Republicans." Big laugh. Easing of tension.

"Senator McGovern," a voice booms through the telephone receiver. McGovern jumps. Electricians have overcompensated. Candidate recovers. "Yes, this is Senator McGovern. I'm ready for your question." Long pause—nervous sounding voice, "Uh, well, uh, Senator, uh, what is your—uh—opinion about marijuana?"

Now anyone at this point in the campaign who doesn't know Senator McGovern's opinion on marijuana can't possibly have read any newspaper or magazine or listened to a single television station in the last 9 months. Whoever is on the line probably had to be helped to dial.

And so it went, stupid question after stupid question while George McGovern sat and patiently answered and smiled and held that ridiculous gray telephone receiver, and must have wondered somewhere through it all why he had ever, ever wanted to be President.

A lot of his aides were wondering too. "It's probably impossible now for McGovern to win," said Larry O'Brien, "but perhaps it's still possible for the Democrats to win or for Nixon to lose." It was now imperative for McGovern to identify himself in the voter's eyes with the Democratic Party and, at the same time, point out the Republican Party's (Nixon's) policy failures. He needed strong television and radio commercials. But here came another struggle between the in-from-the-start crowd and his other aides. Charles Guggenheim had done some fine television spots for the primaries, showing McGovern as the man who was honest and who listened and cared.

But now after such fluffs as Eagleton and Salinger, that "listener" image was no longer just the thing. Instead, McGovern needed to prove he could take charge, that he was Presidential timber. Guggenheim's spots, McGovern's staff people concluded, made the Candidate seem weak and namby-pamby; they merely confirmed the voter's doubts. What was needed were tough issue spots and a clear message to the waverers —Come back to the Party. But Guggenheim refused to change his commercials, and McGovern refused to force him. Unfortunately, Merv Weston, who had loyally pumped his own money into advertising and commercials for McGovern during the early primaries, could no longer be tapped for help. He had been rewarded in usual campaign style by being shoved out entirely after the convention.

Only by ignoring McGovern completely and working on their own were several aides finally able to get new commercials produced by an independent New York producer; and then only after an enormous battle with Guggenheim did they manage to get them aired—the last week of the campaign when it was much, much too late.

The next week I traveled on the Zoo plane—with its cabin decorated with bright orange and black Halloween streamers, hanging rows of keys accumulated from 3 months of campaign hotels, and posters of Nixon ("Would you buy a used car from this man?"). But in this last week, the mood aboard all the planes was changing from giddy optimism to uncanny serenity, the sort of calm which takes over when one finally accepts the presence of a terminal disease.

It might seem that such a realization facing us all would have increased camaraderie, bound us together on our slowly sinking ship. Not so with the McGovern staff, which, as usual, reasoned that the best thing to do on a sinking ship was to systematically push the women and children overboard and fight each other for the Captain's Lounge.

It happened on the runway in Cincinnati. I sensed trouble when I saw Angel and Judy (the girl who had removed me from her Washington apartment after Frank had given it to me) huddled together under a 727 jet wing. They had been engaged in the customary bumping routine. So far, I had not been picked, but now I was.

216 ☐

"Kristi," said Angel, cruising up to me with an endearing smile, "the planes are very full, and I'm terribly sorry but we have to bump someone from the staff."

"There are 11 empty seats," I said, in a routine I now had memorized with the exception of inserting the appropriate number for the day. And, having already planned for this contingency, I went on. "Not only are there 11 empty seats, but I'm not sitting in any of them. I'm sharing a seat with an Oricon TV camera whose seat is paid for by its television station."

Her expression changed. "Well, there just isn't enough room," she said, scowling, "so I'd like you to leave."

"No," I said, trying out the word for the first time. I smiled an Angel-type smile. "You don't seem to like me very much," I said, "but if you can hang on four more days, the campaign will be over."

"Like you?" Angel screamed, echoing my words, her reddened face dissolving into a mass of frowns and wrinkles. "I hate you! I've always hated you!" She caught her breath, gasped, and started to cry. "It's not fair," she sobbed. "It's never been fair. I do all the work and you make five times as much salary as I do!"

Now this was silly. I made no salary at all, a salient fact I attempted to point out. It was useless. Angel was as coherent as a goldfish in a bubble bath. Crying uncontrollably, she fled back to the plane.

I felt considerably unnerved as the TV camera and I settled back into our seat on the Zoo plane. But I wasn't alone. George McGovern was getting unnerved, too. At the next stop in Battle Creek, Michigan, annoyed by a particularly vicious heckler, mild-mannered George suddenly leaned over and whispered in the man's ear, "I've got a secret for you—kiss my ass!"

□ *217*

"It took us twenty-six weeks to find our slogan," muttered a campaign aide. McGovern's remark was heard only by the heckler and several newsmen; by morning, only the smallest suburban weekly had missed the story.

"Well, what can a Democrat say," laughed Frank, "kiss my elephant? Anyway, it solved the Gay Liberation problem—fifty of them are off to do it!"

Back in Washington, even Henry Kimelman was having his bumping problems. According to Billy Cobbs, one of Mankiewicz' assistants, Kimelman had thought it would be nice to bring himself, his wife, and five friends along for the last 2 days of the campaign. No, said Steve Robbins. I won't pay for the plane unless you give me the seats, said Kimelman. No, said Robbins again. You're fired, said Kimelman. I'm not, said Robbins, and Robbins won the round, if not the battle. We may not have been paying the staff or our campaign bills, but somewhere Henry Kimelman was able to scrape up enough money to charter his own plane, and off he roared with his friends to join the happy traveling campaign in its final few days.

Things were definitely going downhill. On the morning after my encounter with Angel in Cincinnati, I got aboard the press bus outside our Michigan hotel for the trip to the Grand Rapids airport and sat down on a seat in front of two McGovern staff workers from the local campaign office. The bus palpitated but did not move. We sat. And sat. Seeing that we were going nowhere, I finally got off to say hello to a friend from *New York Magazine*. I should have stayed on the bus. When I got back on and we finally pulled away, I noticed that three things were missing—the two McGovern staff members and my camera.

"I thought they were friends of yours," said a reporter sitting across the aisle. "I saw them bending over your seat but I thought they were looking for a schedule."

And the day did not improve. We flew to Chicago for a black rally, a less than successful event succinctly characterized by Gordon Weil, "Just like all our black rallies—half white and half empty," from there to a torchlight parade in the rain, and then to a big indoor rally with Mayor Daley. When it was over, a friend from NBC invited me to dinner, and we climbed into a cab. When we arrived at the restaurant, I jumped out, clutching another friend's borrowed camera, and the cab vanished into the rainy night. Only then did I realize that my handbag was on the seat.

Besides my wallet, press card, driver's license, checkbook, credit cards and address book, I had also lost in the bag my flashgun, my wide-angle lens, and eight rolls of film. My photo career was temporarily over. So was my credit, and with the exception of a tag hanging around my neck that said "Witker–Staff," my entire identity.

"Oh, well," said my friend, trying to cheer me up. "Think how much worse it could be. This way at least you don't have to buy airline tickets or worry about identification, and eventually you'll get back to Washington on the campaign plane. Think if you were stranded here in Chicago—alone without the campaign —with no money and no way to write a check or charge an airline ticket. What would you do then?"

I faced that problem 12 hours later. "We're bumping

you off the plane today and it's final," said Angel, fortified by Judy standing next to her. "Some actresses want to come along."

I was too depressed to argue. As Angel in one corner of the room was ejecting me from the plane, George McGovern in another was holding an impromptu press conference, making a desperate plea to the American people not to believe President Nixon's Vietnam peace message. "I just want to warn the American people not to buy this Nixon line. He has no plan for ending this war . . . Don't be fooled by an American President who time after time has put the survival of President Thieu ahead of our prisoners of war . . . Don't let this man trick you. . . ."

McGovern looked weary and almost totally gray, in suit and face, just the way I felt. We had all been fooled; we had all been tricked. What did any of it matter anymore?

The press conference ended and everyone began to drift down the stairs toward the palpitating press buses in front of the hotel. They all seemed to be walking in pairs like animals to the Ark, but one animal was standing on the shore. Somehow, I wanted the whole scene to freeze: the reporters coming down the stairs, the buses throbbing outside. As long as they all stayed in their places, everything was all right. It was just like every day, I was still part of the group. But once they left, I would be entirely alone—abandoned.

Then slowly, the buses filled up, the last stragglers calling to me to hurry, not knowing I had nothing to hurry to, and adding to my feeling of isolation. I envied them, staying with the family which we had become, traveling together, sharing the same experiences, conversations, and thoughts.

220 □

The first bus pulled out, then the second, and finally, the third; and then, I could no longer bear to look at the hotel door or listen to the fading sounds of shifting bus gears. Where a moment before the Sherman House had been *our* hotel, filled with friends wearing familiar octagonal red and white "McGovern Press" tags and piles of equally familiar-looking tagged luggage, now it was an alien hotel lobby with portly men in scarred leather chairs smoking cigars and blank-faced bellboys scurrying around the main desk. The lobby suddenly, seemed cavernous in size and eerily quiet. I felt like a small child lost in a department store—only no one was ever coming to claim me.

The taxi lost and found department was not open on Saturday, but according to the inspector I called, it made no difference. My chances of recovering my pocketbook in the city of Chicago, he pointed out with what turned out to be alarming accuracy, were about the same as my chance of discovering a $1,000 bill in a telephone book (or getting paid on the McGovern campaign). I had been able to borrow ten dollars from one friendly reporter as he hurried onto the bus but it would hardly get me to Washington or New York and, without credit cards, checks, or a single piece of identification, it seemed unlikely that I would be able to charge an airline ticket anywhere. There was no point in calling Mother. So I spent the day in the phone booth calling other people—the weekend clerks at Master Charge, BankAmericard, American Express, Uni-card and Bloomingdale's, to cancel my credit cards; the New York Department of Motor Vehicles which was closed; my New York bank which was closed; and my New York landlady whom I instructed to change my apartment locks (my keys having also been in the bag)—for a nice total of about $25 billed to my New York telephone number, not to mention $30 for the locks.

The other thing I did was to fill out my absentee ballot which I'd been carrying around for several weeks. I had already filled in my choices for Congressman, Assemblyman, State Senator, and Judge—that was easy—but there was this certain area at the very top of the columns which I couldn't seem to fill out—President and Vice President. This ballot is invalid if tampered with, erased, ground up, chewed, etc., read an ominous instruction, which meant I couldn't change my mind.

At least six times, my hand clutching a pen had wafted over that long page, but I couldn't make the final mark. I needed a third option; the ballot as it was offered no possibility of voting *for* McGovern and against his staff.

Like diving into a Maine lake in April, the only way to do it was fast. Concentrating on the names George McGovern and Sargent Shriver and nothing else, I finally checked the Democratic column and quickly pushed the sheet into an Air Mail, Special Delivery envelope. It was done.

By afternoon it occurred to me that the only thing I could possibly do was to rejoin the campaign, which had gone to Texas and Arkansas before stopping in St. Louis. My ten dollars would get me to the airport. Then I would need $28 for the flight to St. Louis, and $28 was borrowable, even from a total stranger.

The reason I thought $28 a borrowable sum was that a total stranger had once borrowed that exact amount from me.

"You won't believe this," a pretty young girl in her

early twenties had said, coming up to me on a New York sidewalk a couple of years before, "but I lost $28 on the train coming in from Westchester, and I desperately need to take the shuttle to Boston where my parents are meeting me."

She had looked so honest (and I had been so rich, having $35 in my wallet that day) that I had given her the money and my New York address for mailing the check so she would "send off immediately" and that was the last I had ever seen of the girl or the $28. "It's the oldest line in the world," friends had told me afterwards.

Well, hopefully someone in the ticket line at the Chicago airport hadn't heard it yet.

I looked over the line—married couples were too suspicious, the wife would probably go into one of those "don't talk to this hippie kid" routines if I approached them; the three unattached girls looked strictly Youth Fare and just as poor as I. But there was one single man with that comfortable in-between look—in-between the country where he might trust strangers and the city where he would not.

I walked up, feeling very criminal and wondering whether this particular terminal had those electric eyes in the ceiling that took pictures of people like me. "You won't believe this," I said, my voice trembling slightly, "but I lost my pocketbook in a taxi and I need $28 to fly to St. Louis to rejoin the campaign, which is the only place anyone knows me because I also lost all my identification."

The man put down his briefcase and scrutinized me. "What campaign?"he asked. Oh God, this would blow it. He wasn't wearing an American flag pin on his lapel but his hair style bordered on crewcut.

"Mc-, uh," I stammered, "McNixon—I mean, uh, McGovern."

There was a period of silence while several people pushed ahead in line.

"Well," he said, "I think your cause is ridiculous, but your plight is worse. Since I'm already buying one ticket to St. Louis I might as well get two. You can send me a check when you have one." He gave me his business card (and I sent the check the instant I returned to New York).

Without further incident or property loss, I flew to St. Louis and made my way over to the charter end of the airport just as the lights of the circling Zoo plane flashed in the distance. Slowly, the big 727 settled down on the runway and, with a great roar, taxied over to the railing where I stood with the waiting crowd. The plane door was opened, and down the stairs, hauling cameras, trench coats, and typewriters, came a weary band of familiar forms. There was more jet engine noise and over came another friend, the *Dakota Queen,* almost touching wings with Zoo. I was back in the family.

A few days later we were in Sioux Falls, South Dakota, where the chill November wind gusted through wide empty streets. The campaign was almost over.

But not quite. There was still the matter of who stayed in which hotel, the downtown Holiday Inn for McGovern and his family, top staff, top press, top friends, and fat cats (now reduced to tabby cats)—or one of the other less centrally located, less prestigious establishments for less prestigious press and staff. All this was determined by George Cunningham, whose own round form was, of course, firmly entrenched in the downtown Holiday Inn. For once, I had not entrusted myself to George Cunningham or the McGovern staff but had instead, with uncustomary foresight, arranged my own accommodations at the downtown Holiday Inn.

As the reporters and staff straggled up to the registration desk, I detected a grayness of skin, slackness of body, and glassiness of eye not in evidence in the early weeks of the campaign. Finally, the unrelenting months of airplane travel, deadlines, cigarettes, skipped meals, and sleeplessness had taken their collective toll. On this night, the few female reporters, looking considerably aged, collapsed in their rooms alone, while the men drifted off with other men, ties loosened, jackets hung limply over shoulders. I suspected now if one of them were to complain to his wife of his deteriorating mental and physical state, he would be telling the truth.

Election Day dawned crisp and sunny, a good day to vote, the coffee shop waitress said. By 8:30, most of us had boarded buses for the hour's drive to McGovern's hometown, Mitchell, where he and his wife would vote before appearing at Dakota Wesleyan University, George McGovern's alma mater, class of 1940.

A small crowd waited outside the Educational Building of Mitchell's Congregational Church. One elderly man in overalls called out, "I know you can do it, George," and a little girl standing beside him held up a hand-lettered sign: "God loves you and I love you." Maybe so, but I wondered if it would help. Every newspaper predicted a Nixon landslide, the only difference in their articles being the size of the accompanying map with its appropriately shaded areas—"Leaning to McGovern"—white, "Leaning to Nixon"—black. All the maps looked universally black, although a couple of them did show a few white patches in the areas of Wisconsin, Massachusetts, West Virginia, Washington, D.C., and South Dakota.

McGovern shook hands in the crowd and then all the photographers pushed into the tiny room where McGovern would vote. I'd always thought it relatively easy to take a picture of someone entering or leaving a voting booth, and it is, if you happen to be the only photographer around. On this particular morning, however, there were about 30 of us, all trying to stand on the same 14 inches of floor.

My prize-winning photo was taken from the floor at McGovern's feet. It included his knees, the bottom of an enormous scroll-like ballot, and three fingers of his left hand. I imagine he voted for McGovern.

The crowd at Dakota Wesleyan University was warm and friendly, but the mood was a strange mixture of excitement and loss—excitement because here was a man they knew personally who might have become President, and loss because they knew he wouldn't.

Even McGovern, for the first time in all these months, spoke in the past tense. "The novelist Thomas Wolfe once wrote, 'you can't go home again,' " he said. "I'm glad that's not true for Eleanor and me. We can come home here. No matter how things turn out to-night I'll be grateful for the opportunity we had to participate in this campaign. . . ." It seemed that all those grueling months of travel and speeches and all the hopes for victory had now come down to one last hope—to win the home state. I suddenly saw the campaign as a giant arch beginning and ending in South

226 ☐

Dakota. McGovern was genuinely happy and content to be home—I hoped that home didn't disappoint him.

Meanwhile, out there across the country, they were voting . . . voting . . . We drove back to Sioux Falls to a press reception at the Minnehaha Country Club. Even the Secret Service agents seemed to fade back from their charge, leaving McGovern free to mingle with us, and he lingered on his answers to our questions, as though as long as we continued to ask his opinion, the campaign would go on; and as long as it went on, there was still hope. But it couldn't go on. The sun was slowly going down, and it was time to go back to the Holiday Inn.

The gaily decorated hotel lobby and screaming crowd behind barricades came as a shock. I had been resigned to the election being lost but actually, the crowd was right. It wasn't over yet; there were still two more hours before the first returns would start to come in. Maybe . . . Maybe . . .

At 6:15, I returned to my room to pack, take a bath, and put on something festive for the occasion. Tonight was the culmination of nine months' work, and it seemed appropriate to celebrate. I came out of my room at 6:45. "It's all over," said a voice. "What is?" I asked. "The election," said the voice which belonged to a Secret Service agent. "It's a Nixon sweep—all the networks have predicted it."

"What about South Dakota?" I asked.

"Looks bad," he said.

So I'd missed it. Nine months of agony and I hadn't even seen the election. It was over, just like that—no sadness, no happiness, no emotion at all. Except about South Dakota—I felt sad about South Dakota.

Over at the Colisseum, a huge multicolored rainbow

was painted across the azure blue wall behind the stage. I had believed in the rainbow once, but unfortunately, it had never stopped raining.

Now I looked at the crowd, hoping to see tears, concern, acceptance, some human emotion. But the faces were expressionless as though everyone had long since ceased to care. They ate their pretzels, drank their Cokes, and took their Instamatic pictures. They were only here because on Tuesday night, November 7, in Sioux Falls, South Dakota, it was the only show in town.

Long after it was over, after McGovern had given a gracious speech (and Eleanor and the children had cried, and I had cried inwardly for their personal loss and disappointment), I went back to the hotel press room. Some newsmen still typed the last of their stories; but, mostly all the work was done; there was nothing to do but mill around. With McGovern in his moment of crushing defeat were few of his top aides: no Fred Dutton, no Pierre Salinger, no Rick Stearns, Harold Himmelman, Eli Segal, or Gary Hart. Even Frank Mankiewicz only pulled in on one of Kimelman's charters as McGovern was leaving the hotel to deliver his concession speech. Said Ted Van Dyk when it was over, "I've never been so humiliated and in the presence of such stupidity in my whole life as in this campaign."

Everyone felt awkward, even our stewardesses who had made up small white buttons imprinted with a red-lettered "Zoo" for those of us who had made our home on the second plane. The family was breaking up and I felt sorry for those I'd liked who had really tried and cared, and suddenly even for those family members I hadn't liked.

Angel and Judy walked by still carrying their lists. "I'm sorry," I said. They looked at each other nervously.

228 ☐

They were down to their last hurrah, the plane trip home, and off to the side of the press room, they went to huddle, crossing off this name, adding that, crossing off this one . . . It seemed totally absurd, like taking reservations for the lifeboat after the ship had sunk.

But it was a habit not to be broken and this was their last hold on power. I bumped myself from the final flight; it would have been incongruous to end it any other way, and the following morning left for the airport and a commercial flight back to Washington just as workmen took down the "Welcome Sen. McGovern" sign from the Holiday Inn marquee.

I took a taxi back to Barbara Howar's house and found myself cheered by the sounds of the real world—the voices of her children, the refrigerator door closing, the dog barking.

The next morning, I packed up my summer's worth of belongings and, late that afternoon, borrowed some more money and flew back to New York. A mound of mail awaited me at the front door and the phone was ringing. It was Pierre's son, Marc. "Guess what?" he said excitedly, "Dad's just signed an exclusive contract for lots of money for a big article on what really happened inside the McGovern campaign!" "Gee, that's really great," I said.

I turned to the mail, mostly ads. But there was one envelope from the Wilshire Hyatt House in Los Angeles which looked like a bill. It was.

It mentioned a sum of $58,964, next to which were the typed words, "This balance has been due since June." HELP. Even for 2 weeks in costly Southern California, that sounded a bit steep.

But wait, that must be the balance for the whole campaign. After all, George McGovern, Frank Mankiewicz, Gary Hart, Gordon Weil, and several hundred others had stayed there too. Besides, there was another amount typed in parentheses under the $58,964: $323.-90, and next to it my name. But I didn't have $323.90. That was the campaign's bill, not mine.

But stamped at the bottom were the words "This bill has been referred back to individuals by the McGovern Finance Committee."

Frank Mankiewicz did not lie. It was a once-in-a-lifetime experience.